MARINE ARCHAEOLOGY:
A HANDBOOK

⊞
ENGLISH HERITAGE

Council for British Archaeology

MARINE ARCHAEOLOGY: A HANDBOOK

Virginia Dellino-Musgrave

CBA Practical Handbook No. 20
Council for British Archaeology 2012

Published in 2012 by the Council for British Archaeology
St Mary's House, 66 Bootham, York, YO30 7BZ

British Library cataloguing in Publication Data
A catalogue record for this book is available from the British Library
ISBN 978-1-902771-91-5

Typeset by Carnegie Book Production
Printed and bound by Lavenham Press Ltd

The publisher acknowledges with gratitude a grant from English Heritage towards the
cost of publication

Front cover: Recording work in progress on the 17th-century Swash Channel Protected
Wreck Site, near the entrance to Poole Harbour, Dorset (Crown copyright; image
courtesy of English Heritage)
Back cover: above: Presence of ship worm (*Teredo navalis*) in part of the remains of the
Flower of Ugie wreck in the eastern Solent (Image courtesy of HWTMA)
below: Point cloud image of the British cargo ship *Rotherfield*, sunk as a blockship in
Scapa Flow, Orkney in 1914 (Crown copyright, Historic Scotland; image produced by
Wessex Archaeology)

Contents

Figures

Acknowledgements

The idea of publishing a Marine Handbook started in English Heritage around 2003. In 2004 Mark Dunkley took over responsibility for the Marine Handbook when he joined English Heritage. In 2005, while Vir Dellino-Musgrave was working for English Heritage, she undertook this project until a move to the Hampshire and Wight Trust for Maritime Archaeology (HWTMA) in November 2007. A year later, English Heritage asked the HWTMA to provide a brief proposal to write a Marine Handbook, to be published by the Council for British Archaeology (CBA). This handbook has been produced with the support and encouragement of English Heritage.

Thanks to all the HWTMA staff for their support and contributions which made this handbook possible, especially Julian Whitewright, who wrote Chapter 4 and undertook all work related to the images presented in this handbook; Kathryn Dagless, who proofread the whole volume; Rachel Bynoe, for contributions on prehistoric submerged landscapes; Amanda Bowens, for her input on Chapter 2; and Julie Satchell, who commented on the draft text.

We are also very grateful to Ian Oxley, Mark Dunkley, Ed Salter, Phil Robertson, Andy Liddell, Kieran Westley, Stephen Fisher, Lucy Blue, Jesse Ransley, Olivia Merritt, Paola Palma, Ben Barton, Dave Hooley, Helen Keeley and Catrina Appleby for their contributions and comments.

Abbreviations

ACHWS	Advisory Committee on Historic Wreck Sites
AcoP	Approved Code of Practice
ADS	Archaeology Data Service
ALSF	Aggregates Levy Sustainability Fund
AMAAA	Ancient Monuments and Archaeological Areas Act
AMAP	Area of Maritime Archaeological Potential
BMAPA	British Marine Aggregate Producers Association
BSAC	British Sub-Aqua Club
CARN	Core Archaeological Record Index
CBA	Council for British Archaeology
CZAS	Coastal Zone Assessment Survey
DBA	desk-based assessment
DCLG	Department for Communities and Local Government
DCMS	Department for Culture, Media and Sport
DEFRA	Department for Environment, Food and Rural Affairs
DfT	Department for Transport
DOENI	Department of the Environment (Northern Ireland)
E&O	education and outreach
EEZ	Exclusive Economic Zone
EIA	Environmental Impact Assessment
ELC	European Landscape Convention
EMEC	European Marine Energy Centre
HER	Historic Environment Record
HMAO	Historic Monuments and Archaeological Objects (Northern Ireland) Order
HSC	Historic Seascape Characterisation
HSE	Health and Safety Executive
HWTMA	Hampshire & Wight Trust for Maritime Archaeology
ICOMOS	International Council on Monuments and Sites
IfA	Institute for Archaeologists
JNAPC	Joint Nautical Archaeology Policy Committee
MAG	Maritime Affairs Group
MCA	Maritime and Coastguard Agency
MCAA	Marine and Coastal Access Act
MCZ	Marine Conservation Zone
MHWS	mean high water spring
MLWS	mean low water spring
MMO	Marine Management Organisation

MOD	Ministry of Defence
MoRPHE	*Management of Research Projects in the Historic Environment*
MPA	Marine Protection Area
MPS	Marine Policy Statement
MSA	Merchant Shipping Act
M(S)A	Marine (Scotland) Act
NAS	Nautical Archaeology Society
NHA	National Heritage Act
NHPP	National Heritage Protection Plan
NIEA	Northern Ireland Environment Agency
NISMR	Northern Ireland Sites and Monuments Record
nm	nautical miles
NMR	National Monuments Record (see also NRHE)
NRHE	National Record of the Historic Environment
OASIS	Online Access to the Index of Archaeological Investigations
PADI	Professional Association of Diving Instructors
PMRA	Protection of Military Remains Act
PPG	Planning Policy Guidance
PPS	Planning Policy Statement
PWA	Protection of Wrecks Act
RAE	Research Assessment Exercise
RCAHMS	Royal Commission on the Ancient and Historical Monuments of Scotland
RCAHMW	Royal Commission on the Ancient and Historical Monuments of Wales
RCZAS	Rapid Coastal Zone Assessment Surveys
RO	Registered Organisation
RoW	Receiver of Wreck
SAA	Sub-Aqua Association
SCUBA	Self-Contained Underwater Breathing Apparatus
SEA	Strategic Environment Assessment
SMP	Shoreline Management Plan
SMR	Sites and Monuments Record (now known as *HER*)
SPP	Scottish Planning Policy
UAD	Urban Archaeological Database
UKCS	UK Continental Shelf
UKHO	United Kingdom Hydrographic Office
UN	United Nations
UNCLOS	United Nations Convention on the Law of the Sea
UNESCO	United Nations Educational, Scientific and Cultural Organisation

CHAPTER 1

The marine historic environment

Our land (and seas) are patterned with its past and it is a pattern of great complexity that grows daily more complex. This pattern tells us not only about our country but also about ourselves.

(Connah 1993)

1.1 Introduction and scope

The aim of this book is to enable popular access to information regarding the marine historic environment: information generally found in academic books or journals which are not necessarily accessible to all. It focuses on discussing key issues regarding marine archaeology in the UK. The coastal zone and the littoral (intertidal) zone between mean low water spring (MLWS) and mean high water spring (MHWS) tides are outside the scope of this book. However, it is acknowledged that there is a clear overlap between 'coastal' and 'marine' areas, and their boundaries should not restrict the understanding of past human activities.

This volume is aimed at a wide audience, including the informed reader, interested amateurs, and non-marine archaeologists – in other words, at any readers with an interest in the historic environment. It complements other popular books such as *Archaeology underwater: the NAS guide to principles and practice* (Bowens 2008), and *Maritime archaeology* (Muckelroy 1978). Importantly, it contributes towards the 'puzzle' defined as maritime archaeology (see below) and provides information crucial to enabling the understanding of archaeology (as a whole) in the UK.

1.2 Structure of the book

This handbook is divided into six chapters. The present chapter introduces the subject and provides a context from which the other chapters develop. It discusses how marine archaeology fits within archaeology as a discipline and its development through time, as well as the extent of the UK marine zone.

Chapter 2 discusses the main sectors involved in marine archaeology, the key areas of work on which they are concentrating, and issues and challenges which they are currently facing. Chapter 3 discusses some of the basic steps followed by professional archaeologists on marine projects, with particular focus on two main types of projects: research-led and development-led projects. The former result from specific, targeted research questions, while the latter stem from developments in the marine or coastal zone such as aggregate extraction or wind-farm construction. Both produce important, albeit different, forms of data which can contribute to our further understanding of the past. Chapter 4 presents some basic information on administration, formal policy, and the legal context relating to the protection and management of underwater cultural heritage within the UK. The main aim of this chapter is to provide a first port of call for those requiring general guidance on this often complicated subject. Chapter 5 summarises the principal international conventions that relate to underwater cultural heritage and have been acknowledged or ratified by the UK. Particular emphasis is placed on the Council of Europe's European Landscape Convention (ELC), since it bridges all components of the historic environment, from land to maritime contexts. Finally, Chapter 6 reflects on some of the key issues explored throughout the book.

1.3 Definitions

To help the reader, this section defines the terminology and concepts that are considered relevant within the context of this book.

1.3.1 How many 'archaeologies'?

The 'traditional' differentiation of maritime, underwater, nautical, and marine archaeology has been continuously debated during the development of archaeology focused on submerged material culture (eg Muckelroy 1978, 9–10). This section briefly defines what is understood by these terms and by the marine historic environment and its components.

In this book, maritime archaeology is understood as the 'big umbrella' which encompasses underwater, nautical, and marine archaeology. Maritime archaeology is the study of material remains relating to human action on seas, interconnected waterways, and adjacent coastal areas (Adams 2002). This includes sites that are not underwater but are related to maritime activities, such as lighthouses, port constructions or shore-based whaling stations, among many others. Underwater archaeology refers to the environment in which the practice of archaeology is undertaken, which can include any type of archaeological remains and sites that are now submerged or partially submerged (eg Bowens 2008, 5–6). Nautical archaeology, like maritime archaeology, can include sites that are not underwater but that are related to ships and shipbuilding, including ship burials, shipwreck remains in the terrestrial environment or shipbuilding yards (*ibid*). The term 'marine' is derived from the Latin *marinus* (of the sea) and, used as an adjective, it means 'of, or relating to, the sea'. Therefore, in this book, marine archaeology relates specifically to cultural remains within the marine (saltwater) environment, including its study and interpretation (see also Dellino-Musgrave 2006, 22–3; Flatman & Staniforth 2006, 168–9).

These terms are used in this book for explanatory purposes in defining an area of research within archaeology, rather than as separate entities (see Adams 2002; Dellino-Musgrave 2006; Staniforth 2003). The main goal of archaeology is to understand the human past, whether the research is undertaken in prehistoric, historic, submerged or terrestrial contexts. 'What can be different are the physical environment, field techniques and classes of material culture analysed where the archaeological discipline is put into practice' (Dellino-Musgrave 2006, 23). Archaeologists study the human past whether its material expression is found on land or underwater, and the discipline involving this study is archaeology itself.

1.3.2   The historic environment

In this book, the 'historic environment' is defined as including 'both the natural and human-made environments (often overlapping) and heritage above- and below-ground, as well as under the sea, that has cultural value and significance worthy of sustainable management and conservation' (Embree & Stevens 2005, 3).

The term 'historic asset' is used for any component of the historic environment (see English Heritage 2008; English Heritage 2001), including, for example, submerged prehistoric landscapes, millennia of shipping wreckage, and crashed aircraft.

1.3.3   The UK marine zone

1.3.3.i   Marine zones

The United Nations Convention on the Law of the Sea (UNCLOS), adopted at the United Nations General Assembly in 1982, was established in an attempt to resolve disputes over access to various parts of the oceans (UN 1983). UNCLOS allows for the recognition of four main marine zones:

- Territorial Waters extending twelve miles from a state's maritime baseline
- an Exclusive Economic Zone (EEZ) extending 200 miles from the coastal state's maritime baseline (or to a median line equidistant from it and any neighbouring coastal state less than 400 miles away)
- the continental shelf which extends from the territorial sea to the deep sea-bed at the outer edge of the continental margin
- the High Seas zone beyond the EEZ's national limits

Each of these marine zones is discussed in detail in Chapter 5. However, it is worth noting here that the UK acceded to UNCLOS, which came into force in

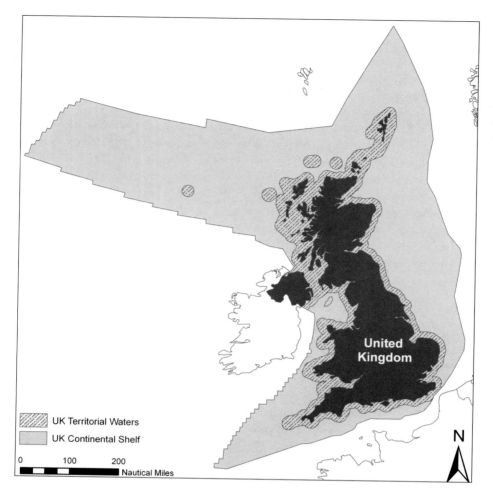

Figure 1.1 Map illustrating the extent of UK territorial waters and UK-controlled continental shelf waters (Image courtesy of HWTMA)

1994. Accordingly, the breadth of sea claimed by the UK as territorial sea is twelve nautical miles (nm) and, though currently not claiming an EEZ, the UK claims what is known as the UK Controlled Waters, which extend for 200nm (Fig 1.1).

1.3.3.ii Landward extent

For the purposes of this book, the landward limit of the marine zone occurs at the level of MLWS. This level is calculated as the average of the low water heights occurring at the time of spring tides. It should be noted that MLWS is an arbitrary datum that is subject to natural change.

1.3.3.iii Ownership of the territorial seabed

The Crown Estate owns around 55% of the foreshore and approximately half of the beds of estuarine areas and tidal rivers in the UK. It also owns the majority of the seabed out to the 12nm territorial limit, including the rights to explore and exploit the natural resources of the UK continental shelf (excluding hydrocarbons such as oil, gas, and coal).

The Crown Estate dates back to 1066, when all English land belonged to William 'in right of The Crown' when he became king following the Norman Conquest. The Sovereign's estates have always been used to raise revenue and, following The Crown Estate Act of 1961, the estate is managed by a Board who have a duty to maintain and enhance the value of the estate and the return obtained from it.

The foreshore is managed by seven regional managing agents, mainly firms of Chartered Surveyors, which carry out negotiations and transactions on behalf of The Crown Estate. The seabed is managed directly by in-house staff of The Crown Estate, with an external minerals agent appointed for the aggregates business. Leases of easement for pipelines and cables, and royalties from the extraction of minerals, principally marine aggregates, are the main sources of revenue from the marine area of the Estate, although revenue from offshore renewables is expected to grow significantly over the coming years.

The Crown Estate's role is as a landowner, while the decision as to whether activities such as aggregate extraction are permitted is taken by the UK government. The Department for Transport (DfT) and the Department for Communities and Local Government introduced a statutory licensing procedure in 1989 to replace the non-statutory Government View Procedure introduced in 1968.

1.3.3.iv Traditional rights

There is a public right of fishery in UK tidal waters that does not discriminate between persons or classes of persons and generally extends to all species of sea fish. The UK fisheries authorities have legal powers to regulate this public right in terms of, for example, the removal of certain species and the use of certain types of fishing gear in particular sea areas.

Additionally, centuries-old common law has established that there is a public right of navigation for vessels in the tidal reaches of many rivers, that anchoring in the course of navigation is part of the public right and that, when the tide is in, there is an absolute right to navigate through the water (although not necessarily a right to land a boat or launch one). It is not possible, therefore, to fence off foreshore areas, as this would limit navigation. Where applicable, harbour authorities may exercise a degree of control over navigation through marine by-laws established and enforced by the authorities to ensure safe navigation within the main shipping channels. These public rights of fishery and navigation need to be respected during the course of archaeological investigations.

1.4 Maritime archaeology *vs* commercial salvage

The salvage of lost ships and cargoes is a profession with a long history, but the recovery of historically/archaeologically important material and the commercial exploitation of the maritime cultural heritage are ethically problematic, albeit lawful, activities in most legal jurisdictions (Bowens 2008). Even so, shipwreck salvage, which relies on the sale and dispersal of shipwreck artefacts and archive material with the motivation to profit from such activity, is not within recognised archaeological best practice (IfA 2010; UNESCO 2001). Archaeological remains are unique and non-renewable resources and, as such, should in the first instance be left *in situ*, unless they are under threat. When *in situ* preservation is not possible, then systematic archaeological research based on a clear project design should be undertaken. The results of such research and any excavation of material remains, if undertaken, should be deposited within a publicly accessible museum or archive to ensure their long-term preservation and curation. Failure to make archives publicly available limits enjoyment by members of the public, study and reinterpretation by researchers, and access for children and educational programmes. Furthermore, the UK government recognises the 2001 UNESCO Convention on the Protection of the Underwater Cultural Heritage Annex as best practice for underwater archaeology and has advocated adherence to the principles of this Annex which are compatible with existing UK legislation (see Chapters 4 and 5). Rule 2 of the Annex states that 'The commercial exploitation of underwater cultural heritage for trade or speculation or its irretrievable dispersal is fundamentally incompatible with the protection and proper management of underwater cultural heritage. Underwater cultural heritage shall not be traded, sold, bought or bartered as commercial goods.' Rule 9 of the Annex requires that 'Prior to any activity directed at underwater cultural heritage, a project design for the activity shall be developed and submitted to the competent authorities for authorization and appropriate peer review' (UNESCO 2001).

1.5 Brief introduction to the history of maritime archaeology

This section discusses the development of maritime archaeology, which can generally be related to the history of diving. Shipwreck archaeology, as part of maritime archaeology, was at first the domain of maritime historians and classical archaeologists (Lenihan 1983, 38). The early development of maritime archaeology was characterised by adventurers rapidly developing diving equipment and techniques that enabled marine exploration. These early times were marked by an emphasis on methodological issues and little development of theoretical approaches (see Babits & Van Tilburg 1998; Barstad 2002; Broadwater 2002; Muckelroy 1978; 1980; Watson 1983, among others). Recently, the situation has changed, with maritime archaeologists developing theoretical frameworks and models that contribute to the interpretation of contextualised past human activities, going beyond site-specific descriptive analysis (Adams 2003; 2006; Dellino-Musgrave 2006).

1.5.1 Diving

1.5.1.i Diving: early development phases

As a product of its time, this early stage of development was focused on traditional salvage activities, with no clear research aims and objectives. In the 16th and 17th centuries diving for salvage purposes was carried out using open bells (see Fig 1.2), from which divers would venture to secure ropes or manipulate various pieces of equipment whilst holding their breath (Watson 1983). The next development phase occurred in the 18th century with the invention of a closed bell-barrel-like construction, which increased the diver's endurance. This is exemplified in Edmund Halley's method of replenishing air underwater in a lead-coated wooden bell, published in 1716 in the 'The Art of Living Underwater or a Discourse concerning the Means of Furnishing air at the Bottom of the Sea, in any Ordinary Depths', in the Royal Society's *Philosophical Transactions*. Frequently considered to be the basis of the modern diving bell, this system made it possible to stay underwater for up to two hours (Delbourgo 2007; Muckelroy 1978, 10–12).

Figure 1.2 Illustration of a simple diving bell (Chambers & Chambers 1881)

The 19th century saw the invention of the first diving dress (see Watson 1983). Standard 19th-century diving dress consisted of a metallic (copper, brass or bronze) diving helmet, an airline or hose from a surface-supplied diving air pump, a canvas diving suit, diving knife and boots. This type of diving equipment is also known as *hard-hat* equipment. During the 1820s the Deane brothers of Deptford, who were maritime antiquarians, patented a 'smoke helmet' for fire fighters. This helmet, fitting over the head and held with weights, was also

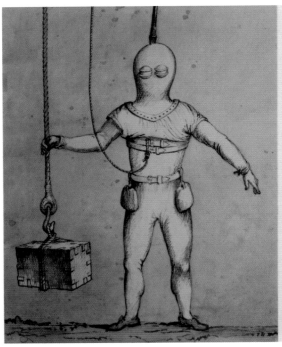

Figure 1.3 Early helmet and diving suit, recorded in a watercolour sketch at Portsmouth Dockyard (*c* 1831) by Simon Goodrich (1773–1847), engineer and mechanist to the Royal Navy (Image courtesy of John Bevan (Bevan 1996, pl 6))

Figure 1.4 Standard diving dress (right) and the 'Tritonia one-atmosphere diving suit' being prepared for a dive in 1935

used for diving. Air was supplied from the surface. By 1828 the Deane brothers were marketing the helmet with a separate 'diving suit', secured to the helmet with straps rather than being attached to it (Fig 1.3). By the late 1830s Augustus Siebe, a German-born engineer who lived in England, sealed the Deane brothers' diving helmet to a watertight, air-containing rubber suit. The closed diving suit connected to an air pump on the surface became the first effective standard diving dress, and the prototype of hard-hat rigs still in use today. Although innovative, this hard-hat diving equipment was costly, bulky, and difficult to use (Fig 1.4).

1.5.1.ii Diving in the 20th century

During the 19th century several lochs in Scotland were drained to provide land for agricultural purposes. This exposed 'crannog mounds' and highlighted the artificial nature of some of these islands. The realisation that these mounds were the remains of ancient dwellings inspired people such as Odo Blundell to carry out limited excavations in Scotland and the Highlands at the beginning of the 20th century (Blundell 1910). Blundell, a Benedictine monk, was the first to investigate a Scottish crannog when he dived in Loch Ness using hard-hat apparatus comprising a helmet, canvas suit, and lead boots (Blundell 1909). Several partial excavations of crannogs were undertaken by Blundell, direct observations made, and finds recorded. Finds of structural timbers, artefacts, and plant materials allowed the formulation of theories about how and why these dwellings were constructed.

During the early 20th century attention was focused principally on classical antiquities and ancient works of art from the Mediterranean: 'While modern archaeology was developing on land, there seemed to be no archaeologists adventurous enough to go under water in the standard diving equipment of the day' (Muckelroy 1978, 11).

In 1923 Yves Le Prieur developed a manually controlled free-flow open-circuit Self-Contained Underwater Breathing Apparatus (SCUBA), which allowed a

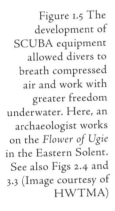

Figure 1.5 The development of SCUBA equipment allowed divers to breath compressed air and work with greater freedom underwater. Here, an archaeologist works on the *Flower of Ugie* in the Eastern Solent. See also Figs 2.4 and 3.3 (Image courtesy of HWTMA)

diver to breathe from a cylinder containing compressed air. With a focus mainly on diving methodology and techniques, rather than on underwater research, in 1943 Jacques-Yves Cousteau and Emile Gagnan invented the first commercially successful automatically controlled open-circuit type of SCUBA diving equipment, the Aqua-Lung. Although there was little progress with maritime archaeology during this time owing to World War II, the possibility of work underwater became real for Cousteau and his Underwater Research Group and for future archaeologists (Muckelroy 1978).

In 1953 the British Sub-Aqua Club (BSAC) was formed in London by a number of 'persons interested in underwater activities' whose aim was 'to promote underwater exploration, science and safety in these activities' (http://www.bsac.com/). The BSAC quickly became a significant force in sport diving and by the end of 1954 it had been recognised in Britain as the governing body for the new sport of underwater swimming, a responsibility which it still retains. Sport diving made marine historic assets accessible: professional archaeologists learnt to dive (Fig 1.5) and divers learnt to apply archaeological techniques, helping to develop maritime archaeological research and practice.

The body that eventually became the Nautical Archaeology Society (NAS) was originally incorporated and registered as a charity in 1972 under the name (The) Nautical Archaeology Trust Limited. The Trust was reconstituted in 1986 as the NAS mainly to oversee the production of the *International Journal of Nautical Archaeology* (see Bowens 2008, 1). Today, the NAS is dedicated to advancing education in nautical archaeology at all levels, with a particular focus on volunteer training for both divers and non-divers. Through this work it contributes to improving techniques in excavating, conservation, and reporting as well as encouraging the participation of members of the public at all stages. Initiatives such as this have led to a raised awareness of the unique and fragile nature of historic assets as well as promoting understanding, caring, and enjoyment of them.

Further information on the development of diving is available from the Historical Diving Society, which was formed in 1990 to promote interest in, and awareness of, the history of underwater exploration (http://www.thehds.com).

1.5.2   Developing maritime archaeology

The development of maritime archaeology as a discipline can be traced back to the 19th century. It was then that Charles Lyell, a pioneer in geology, argued that the present is the key to the past (Lyell 1830–33; reprinted 2005). He introduced the concept of stratigraphy utilised today in archaeological studies, and recognised the presence of archaeological remains in the marine environment (*ibid*, 318–34). Despite this recognition, maritime archaeology in general, and underwater archaeology in particular, has necessarily been guided by technological developments which facilitate underwater exploration which tends to be focused on historic wrecks and site-specific analyses (see Babits & Van Tilburg 1998; Lenihan 1983; Muckelroy 1978; 1980; Ruppé & Barstad 2002). These approaches

have had limited benefit in relation to wider cultural contexts and processes (see Ransley *et al* forthcoming). Recently this situation has started to change, however, with explorations of shipwrecks going beyond traditional approaches and interpreting them as a result of human activities within wider social contexts (see Adams 2003; Dellino-Musgrave 2006; Staniforth 2003).

Importantly, the *Charter on the Protection and Management of Underwater Cultural Heritage*, which was ratified by the 11th ICOMOS General Assembly in 1996, defines underwater cultural heritage as 'the archaeological heritage which is in, on or has been removed from, an underwater environment. It includes submerged sites and structures, wreck sites and wreckage and their archaeological and natural context' (ICOMOS 1998, 183). And, as recent research demonstrates, marine archaeology goes beyond shipwrecks; the seas around Britain contain an immense wealth of archaeological sites and remains (Roberts & Trow 2002), ranging from submerged landscapes, primarily relating to prehistoric periods (see Bates *et al* 2007; Flemming 2004; Gaffney *et al* 2009), to watercraft, aircraft and other structures from early periods to the modern era (eg Wessex Archaeology 2008).

In European archaeology the 1960s and 1970s saw rapid development in methods, techniques, and scientific analysis that has now given way to self-conscious and more theoretically informed enquiry about the identity and goals of professional underwater archaeology (Barstad 2002, 4–6; Watson 1983, 24–7). During this period, shipwrecks started to be considered as an archaeological phenomenon – as important and unique documents of the human past (eg Bass 1966). Despite Muckelroy's last work being undertaken in 1980, his research, ideas, and methods of explaining material culture continue to have a significant impact on current maritime archaeological practice. He was the first to define maritime archaeology as 'the scientific study of the material remains of man and his activities on the sea' (Muckelroy 1978, 4). He also introduced systematic research with a strong 'processual' and explicit theoretical framework. His primary concerns were to explain archaeological problems and to understand human past activities, rather than simply to describe objects recovered from shipwrecks or any other submerged archaeological site (Muckelroy 1978).

In the UK this period is exemplified by the exploratory research carried out on the protected wreck site of the *Mary Rose*, a warship that sank in 1545 in the Solent (Fig 1.6). This work was undertaken by Alexander McKee, a maritime author, historian, and explorer, who continued performing exploratory dives until 1979, when the Mary Rose Trust was formed. Subsequently a full programme of work was developed to excavate, survey, and empty the hull and then refloat it ashore for study, conservation, and display (see Bradford 1982; Marsden 2003). This programme was original in that it was undertaken via controlled and systematic methods based on a research design with clear aims and objectives, justifying how and why the work was going to be performed.

In maritime archaeology the concept of a 'time-capsule' or 'Pompeii premise' repeatedly arises (see Adams 2001), while such topics as post-depositional processes and the environmental dynamics of the area under study are often neglected. The 'Pompeii premise' assumes that a given archaeological site was 'frozen' in a single day in time, with wreck sites thus considered as representative of a specific event, the shipwreck, disregarding other cultural and natural factors that may alter their formation and subsequent presentation (see Martin 1997; Muckelroy 1978; Parker 1995). Consequently, especially from the 1960s to 1990s and even occasionally today, many underwater sites have been presented as a descriptive entity; theoretical issues have been avoided and micro-scales of analysis focused simply on the description of wreck sites and their contents have been used. For example, in the UK during the 1980s controlled and systematic work via a research design was undertaken in the protected wreck site the *Amsterdam*, a Dutch East India Company vessel that sank into the beach sands near Hastings in 1749 (Fig 1.7). Although descriptive and methodologically orientated, the work undertaken on the *Amsterdam* combined different sources of evidence, including historical documentation, as well as comparative archaeological material.

Equally, particular events can be used to explore larger-scale issues of cultural change and continuity and social processes. It is when that event, at an archaeological level, is incorporated into a larger scale of analysis that the potential of maritime archaeology, with some of its most powerful explanatory value, can be realised. It therefore becomes necessary to expand the horizon imposed on the event itself if archaeologists wish to gain a better and more comprehensive understanding of past human activities.

In the 1990s the concepts of maritime cultures and maritime cultural

Figure 1.7 The Dutch
East Indiaman
Amsterdam was driven
ashore at Bulverhythe,
near Hastings, in
1749, after the crew
mutinied. The
remains of the vessel
are one of the UK's
designated protected
shipwrecks (Image
courtesy of Peter
Marsden)

landscapes arose. The concept of 'maritime cultures' was explored as a set of norms relating to the maritime world and encompassing certain groups or communities (Parker 1995, 92). The idea of a 'maritime cultural landscape' was introduced by Westerdahl, who understood it as referring to remnants of maritime culture on land as well as underwater (Westerdahl 1992, 5; Westerdahl 1994; also see Parker 2001, 23–6). The introduction of these concepts made archaeologists reflect on the social significance of material remains as well as considering more integrative approaches to land and sea: issues that are flourishing in the 21st century.

This period also introduced the exploration of ship- and boat-building traditions as social practices, recognising that the building traditions within which 'the vessel is constructed will embody a system of ideas about what boats and ships are and how they should be designed and constructed' (Adams 2001, 301–2; also see McGrail 1995).

The notion of the ship as a symbol was also developed during the 1990s. This idea was based on the assumption that material culture is meaningfully constituted and is not a simple reflection of how society is organised (Hodder 1982; 1991; Tilley 1989; 1990). The ship as a symbol is therefore considered as 'ideology afloat': an expression of social ideas, including those aspects of the tradition within which the vessel was constructed and those that influenced choices in the production and consumption processes (see Adams 2001; 2003).

During the 21st century the emphasis of maritime-archaeology-related studies started to shift towards a wider and integrated understanding of maritime-related aspects of the past (eg Adams 2003; 2006; Dellino-Musgrave 2006; Loveluck & Tys 2006; Willis 2009). More importantly, recent research also recognises that archaeological remains of historic and prehistoric human habitation are also present in, on, or under the seabed, highlighting the fact that maritime archaeological concerns go beyond shipwrecks and their cargoes (eg Adams 2002; Dolwick 2008; Flemming 2004; Gaffney *et al* 2009; 2007; Momber *et al* 2009).

As regards the professionalisation of maritime archaeology, from the mid-1980s in the UK maritime research featured in the earliest discussions of the Institute of Archaeologists (IfA, formerly the Institute of Field Archaeologists) and initial standards and guidance were thus developed and agreed (Oxley & O'Regan 2001). There has also been a conscious effort towards raising capacity in the sector as well as engaging new audiences in maritime archaeology, which has led to the development of many educational and outreach initiatives.[1]

1.6   Summary

The development of maritime archaeology has in the main been confined to technological and methodological advances and focused on the analysis of historic wrecks. Recently, a more comprehensive understanding of historic assets, which recognises that archaeological remains of historic and prehistoric human habitation are also present in, on, or under the seabed, has been developed. This has demonstrated that maritime archaeology studies must go beyond shipwrecks and their cargoes.

In general, there has been a lack of theoretically informed approaches aimed at establishing a more integrated understanding of past human activities. However, this situation has changed in recent years, with maritime archaeologists developing theoretical frameworks and models that go beyond site-specific descriptive analysis in contributing to the interpretation of contextualised past human activities.

Lately, educational and outreach initiatives have been developing across the sector, engaging a wide range of audiences. This has contributed to an increased awareness of the marine historic environment and its unique and fragile nature, as well as promoting its understanding for present and future generations.

Endnotes

1   Among others, see www.hwtma.org,uk; www.nauticalarchaeologysociety.org; www.bournemouth.ac.uk/caah/maritimearchaeology/maritime_archaeology.html; www.southampton.ac.uk/archaeology/cma/.

CHAPTER 2

Marine archaeology in the United Kingdom

… archaeology, the investigation of the human past. Our created past surrounds us and it matters.

(Gamble 2001)

It has been recognised that the seas around Britain contain an immense wealth of archaeological sites and remains of all types (see, among others, Flemming 2004; Gaffney *et al* 2007). As an island that has experienced successive waves of settlement over many centuries and as a major naval, mercantile, industrial, and imperial power, Britain's history – and the everyday experience of many of its inhabitants – has been inextricably linked to its surrounding seas. Hence, the variety of work undertaken in this field is immense and advances in the knowledge of our common past feed from the work undertaken by those different sectors who work on the marine archaeology of the UK. Owing to the scope of this book, this chapter does not attempt to summarise the work in marine archaeology that has been undertaken so far. Instead, it focuses on discussing the main areas and issues that are being addressed by different sectors and the principal challenges faced.

This chapter is subdivided into a number of sections that guide the reader through several different subjects and topics, including the main sectors involved in marine archaeology, key topic areas upon which these different sectors are concentrating, and current challenges.

2.1 Main sectors involved in marine archaeology

This section aims to briefly introduce the main sectors involved in marine archaeology in the UK, which can be summarised as follows:

- archaeological contractors
- research institutions, trusts and societies
- curators
- independent groups
- individual divers and salvors

2.1.1 Archaeological contractors

The number of specialist marine archaeological contractors within the UK still remains relatively small. However, these numbers are growing in light of increased marine development. Much of the work in this sector is related to development-led projects or work won through competitive tender. Archaeological contractors act on behalf of developers to ensure that requirements for planning or development consent are fulfilled. Further details on development-led projects are provided in Chapter 3.

2.1.2 Research institutions, trusts and societies

This sector includes universities, charities, and societies which concentrate on the investigation of heritage assets in the marine environment. The sector ranges from those who have a local or regional focus to those who have a national remit.

2.1.3 Curators

This sector relates to heritage agencies and government bodies who have statutory responsibilities for the historic environment. For example, English Heritage is the government's advisory body for the historic environment in England. In Scotland, Historic Scotland advises Scottish Ministers on all aspects of the historic environment and is also responsible for administering devolved heritage protection legislation (eg the designation and licensing of wreck sites in UK territorial waters adjacent to Scotland; further discussed in Chapter 4). In a development-led context curators are consulted on consent applications, for which they provide specific knowledge or advice. The consents process is explained in Chapter 3.

2.1.4 Independent groups

This sector represents the long history of voluntary involvement in maritime and marine archaeology in the UK. There are a number of active local and regional groups, such as the designated historic wreck site licensees, investigating either a single site or a range of sites. Other groups address broader issues mainly related to the profession as a whole; these are exemplified by the IfA's Maritime Affairs Group, discussed further in Chapters 3 and 4.

2.1.5 Individual divers and salvors

This sector is represented through the Receiver of Wreck (RoW) reports. Although these reports are often not part of structured archaeological research, the combined records provide the largest archive of data on objects from the maritime and marine historic environment of the UK.

2.2 Key topic areas

The different sectors involved in marine archaeology have, of course, different remits and interest areas. This section aims to provide a brief overview of the key topic areas in which the different sectors mentioned above are involved. These, possibly in oversimplified form, are as follows:

+ Research
+ Management
+ Development-led work
+ Education and outreach

2.2.1 Research

Archaeology is the study of the past through the material remains that people have left behind. In essence, it comprises three 'things': objects, landscapes/seascapes, and the interpretations of these reached by archaeologists (Gamble 2001, 15). These 'things' are contained within the two inseparable dimensions that archaeologists use to contextualise and interpret the past: space and time. In simple words, space is where objects are and human activities take place, and can be analysed at local (or site-specific), regional, national or international scales of analysis. Time refers to chronologies which, in the case of archaeology, can extend from prehistory to the present day. However, time is also experienced: elements of the past are retained in the present and archaeologists interpret them differently, often changing their perspective about them as their research questions change (see Gamble 2001; Gosden 1994; Tilley 1993). Consequently, archaeologists need to consider the contexts under study and the ways in which these are investigated and interpreted (see Muckelroy 1978). However, in the offshore zone this is not always straightforward because of the dynamic nature of the marine environment.

2.2.1.i Research frameworks

Research frameworks are concerned with the academic advancement of archaeology and are rooted around key overarching-research issues (Olivier 1996, 5). In the UK research frameworks have been developed to stimulate and inform discussions about past and future research into the historic environment. They have provided a coherent strategic framework for the development of research by critically reviewing the current state of archaeological knowledge and considering the potential and practicability of future areas of research. Research frameworks are inclusive, involving participation and consultation from professional, commercial, and voluntary sectors and utilising a breadth of knowledge and experience to set out research priorities.

There are a number of research frameworks that refer to aspects of the marine historic environment. For example, in England the North East Regional Research Framework and the more recent South East Research Framework have considered the marine historic environment. These demonstrate that the marine historic environment is integral to all aspects of the historic environment, ranging from now-submerged elements of prehistoric archaeology to the material culture of ports, as well as networks of communication, trade, and defence (see Petts & Gerrard 2006; http://www.kent.gov.uk/leisure_and_culture/heritage/south_east_research_framework.aspx). Other recently published research frameworks include the *Research and conservation framework for the British Palaeolithic* (Pettitt *et al* 2008), *Metals and metalworking: a research framework for archaeometallurgy* (Bayley *et al* 2008), and *Understanding the workplace: a research framework for industrial archaeology in Britain* (Gwyn & Palmer 2006). These illustrate that, to enable a more comprehensive understanding of past human activities, maritime aspects need to be taken into account when studying or focusing on specific periods or on types of material culture or research areas that could often be perceived as 'terrestrial'.

International initiatives such as the North Sea Prehistory Research and Management Framework have combined effective collaboration between industry and the heritage sector. The North Sea Prehistory Research and Management Framework attempts to consider how future research and management should be directed in the North Sea. This is an area that represents a common European cultural heritage. It is from the North Sea margin that the earliest evidence of a pre-modern human presence in northern Europe has been discovered; the region was inhabited, and also served as a pathway for human migration, for many hundreds of thousands of years (Peeters *et al* 2009).

Recently, the Maritime and Marine Historic Environment Research Framework for England, coordinated by Southampton University and funded by English Heritage, was undertaken. This research framework provides for the first time a coherent overview of research undertaken so far. This will enable long-term strategic planning, inform policy, and provide a statement of agreed research priorities within which researchers can shape and seek funding for projects (Ransley *et al* forthcoming). More importantly, it seeks to provide an inclusive thematic perspective and integrate the offshore marine zone as a whole.[1] Similarly, the Scottish Archaeological Research Framework was set up by the Society of Antiquaries of Scotland, with primary funding from Historic Scotland and support from across the archaeological sector in and beyond Scotland, in order to provide a framework for the development of research in Scottish archaeology by reviewing the current state of archaeological knowledge and considering the potential and practicability of future areas of research.[2]

The Research Framework for the Archaeology of Wales recognises that maritime archaeology is the least studied archaeological resource in Wales. It highlights the need for an improved knowledge of the changes to the coastline over time and of the use of the estuaries and sea for food and transport, which will enable a more comprehensive understanding of past and present settlement within, and exploitation of, the Welsh land mass.[3]

At the time of writing, no research framework is being developed in Northern Ireland. Marine archaeological research is mainly undertaken by the Centre for Maritime Archaeology (University of Ulster) and has concentrated on three

Figure 2.1 Illustration of the fluctuation in mean sea level around the UK between (a) the Last Glacial Maximum and (b) the end of the Palaeolithic/start of the Holocene. Dashed line shows the reconstructed palaeo-shoreline; ice sheets have been omitted for clarity. Reconstructions should be taken as approximations owing to uncertainties regarding eustatic sea-level history, isostatic rebound, shelf erosion and deposition (Image courtesy of Kieran Westley; information used to create reconstructions is from Lambeck 1995, Milne 2002, Shennan *et al* 2006 and Edwards & Brooks 2008)

main areas: foreshore, coastal and freshwater landscapes; shipwrecks; and marine geoarchaeology.[4]

These research frameworks have provided and continue to provide a coherent overview of previous research into the maritime, marine, and coastal archaeology of the UK. This will enable long-term strategic planning by the heritage sector and the UK government, as well as providing a statement of agreed research priorities within which researchers can shape future projects.

2.2.1.ii Marine archaeology: multi-disciplinary and multi-scale

Archaeology is interdisciplinary in nature (interacting with areas of study such as geography, biology, geophysics, and so on) and involves different scales of analysis. This is also the case within an offshore research context.

Within the research institutions, trusts and societies sector, academics are currently addressing broad and interdisciplinary issues. For example, in recent years there has been an emphasis on reconstructing environmental changes using detailed geophysical survey data (Gaffney *et al* 2009) and complex glacial models (Lambeck 1995; Shennan & Andrews 2000) (Fig 2.1). The archaeological and palaeoenvironmental significance of now-drowned landscapes and submerged forests has also been recognised by the research undertaken in submerged forests in the Severn Estuary and Bristol Channel (see Bell *et al* 2009; Hillam *et al* 1990; Nayling & Manning 2007); at Bouldnor Cliff, off the Isle of Wight (Momber

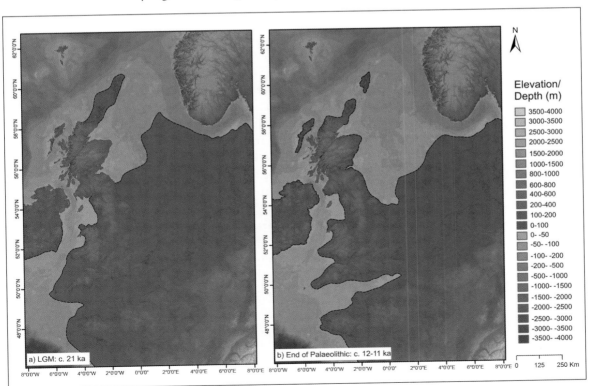

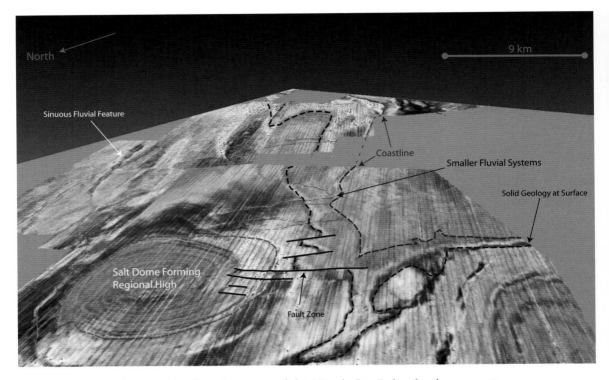

North

9 km

Sinuous Fluvial Feature

Coastline

Smaller Fluvial Systems

Solid Geology at Surface

Salt Dome Forming
Regional High

Fault Zone

2004; 2006; Momber *et al* 2011); and as part of the North Sea Palaeolandscapes Project (Gaffney *et al* 2007; 2009).

The North Sea Palaeolandscapes Project, conducted by Birmingham University, undertook the mapping of the submerged landscape known as Doggerland. It covered over 23,000km² of the English Sector of the North Sea and utilised petroleum industry 3D seismic data. Well-preserved lake beds, rivers and wetland areas have been interpreted (Fig 2.2). For example, the data showed that the Dogger Bank formed an emergent plain during the Holocene with complex meandering river systems and associated tributary or distributary channels and lakes dominating the region (see Gaffney *et al* 2007; 2009). This type of work goes beyond methodological issues, offering the potential to identify and locate palaeoenvironmental deposits associated with prehistoric landscapes (eg the Sussex coast (see Gupta *et al* 2007) and the Irish Sea (Fitch *et al* 2010)).

Dix *et al* (2004) have addressed the particular importance of the nature and scale of palaeogeographic and palaeoenvironmental change to the UK continental shelf (and its margins) in terms of the process of palaeogeographic reconstruction, as it can alter radically over not only prehistoric but also historic timescales (Dix *et al* 2004; Ransley *et al* forthcoming) (Fig 2.3). There is a need, therefore, to understand the nature of the UK continental shelf and its margins, including both the short- and long-term processes that affect them. It is thus clear that interaction with other disciplines, such as palaeogeography (the study of past geographies), can make significant contributions to the understanding of past physical landscapes (now drowned) and their use by contemporary people.

Figure 2.2 Interpretation of buried landscapes in the southern North Sea (Image courtesy of the North Sea Palaeolandscape Project (VISTA, University of Birmingham). This project was funded by the Marine ALSF and administered by English Heritage)

Trusts and societies often address more site-specific research issues which are generally technologically focused and descriptive, concentrating primarily on what has been defined as 'nautical archaeology' (see Chapter 1). These studies still need to be understood within the economic, political, and social transformations of the period (for further details see Ransley *et al* forthcoming). For example, the influence of French ships on English shipbuilding in the eighteenth century is for the most part well understood, yet the interactions between shipbuilding traditions in the new colonies and English shipyards are unexplored (see Dellino-Musgrave 2006; Ransley *et al* forthcoming, Chapter 8). Moreover, these technologically focused and descriptive studies often overlook the fact that the study of local or site-specific issues can provide new insights into broader aspects of the past. A slight shift in emphasis can be seen recently in the archaeological research undertaken by the Hampshire and Wight Trust for Maritime Archaeology (HWTMA) on the *Flower of Ugie*, a wooden vessel sunk in 1852 in the Eastern Solent (Whitewright & Satchell 2011).

The story of the *Flower of Ugie* is more than just the biography of a mid-19th-century British sailing ship (Fig 2.4). Soon after its launch in 1838, the ship's design would have been perceived as old-fashioned. This is because, in the following decades, approaches to the building of large sailing ships were fundamentally altered. These developments took place against a backdrop of rapid expansion in trade routes and levels of connectivity that soon encircled the globe. It is the contextualisation of the vessel within these events that can contribute to modern concerns relating to the future provision for Britain's underwater cultural heritage and its relationship to the continued economic exploitation of the seas around Britain (Whitewright & Satchell 2011, Chapter. 1).

Consequently, it is in the integration of local, regional, national, and international scales of analysis that specific case studies can be contextualised within broader circumstances, thus going beyond descriptive studies. By plying between local and broad scales, archaeology and material culture studies can make a rich contribution to an understanding of how the interplay of people

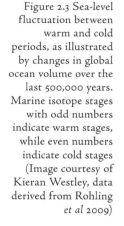

Figure 2.3 Sea-level fluctuation between warm and cold periods, as illustrated by changes in global ocean volume over the last 500,000 years. Marine isotope stages with odd numbers indicate warm stages, while even numbers indicate cold stages (Image courtesy of Kieran Westley, data derived from Rohling *et al* 2009)

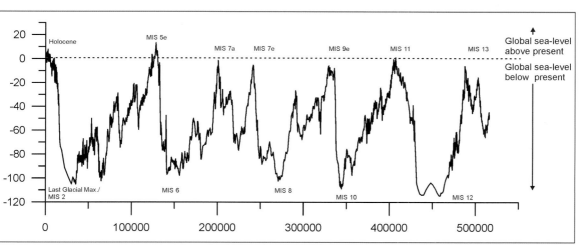

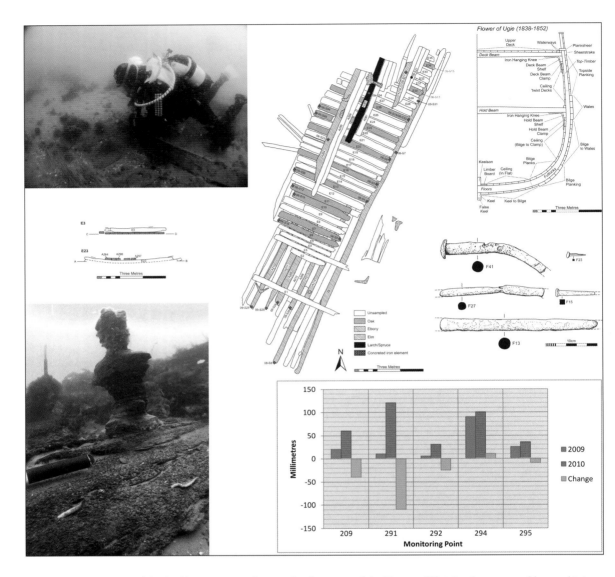

Figure 2.4 A synthesis of the building, use, wrecking and rediscovery of the *Flower of Ugie* has been created by combining archaeological and historical sources and through materials analysis of the extant shipwreck remains. Clockwise from top left: archaeological diver survey; wood species identification; Lloyds Survey Report interpretation; copper and brass bolts sampled for metal analysis; monitoring point observations of sediment change; observed degradation of seabed remains; recorded frame sections. See also Figs 1.5 and 3.3 (Image courtesy of HWTMA)

and objects was driven by interests, motives, and intentions (Gosden & Knowles 2001, xix; Hall 2000, 17–18). More importantly, comparisons with other places and other communities will emphasise the richness and diversity of human experience, deepening our understanding of past societies (see Lawrence 2003).

2.2.2 Management

A priority of the present coalition government is the protection of the nation's cultural heritage (DCMS 2010, 3). In line with this, the UK government's overarching aim is that the historic environment and its heritage assets should be conserved and enjoyed for the quality of life they bring to present and future generations (DCLG 2010, 2). To achieve this, the UK government's objectives are as follows:

- to deliver sustainable development by ensuring that policies and decisions concerning the historic environment recognise that heritage assets are finite and non-renewable;
- to conserve heritage assets in a manner appropriate to their significance;
- to contribute to the knowledge and understanding of the past.

Achieving effective and sustainable management of the historic environment depends on sound principles, clear policies, guidance based on those principles, and the quality of the decisions that stem from their consistent application. An attempt to achieve this is demonstrated by English Heritage's *Conservation Principles, Policies and Guidance* (see English Heritage 2008).

The management of the marine historic environment is mainly focused on:

- preservation *in situ*
- preservation by investigation

Preservation *in situ* means the active preservation of the underwater cultural heritage in its original location (see UNESCO 2001). *In situ* preservation is certainly the preferred approach in the UK; however, underwater sites present challenges in this regard. The underwater environment is very dynamic, and historic assets within this environment can experience ongoing processes of burial, exposure, and reburial. If a site is exposed on the seabed surface biological, chemical, and physical changes in the archaeological material will occur. If a site is exposed, therefore, it is degrading, and it will require active intervention in order to be preserved *in situ* (discussion on this issue is detailed in Ransley 2007). For example, English Heritage recognises that natural processes, such as erosion, cannot always be prevented. However, it is also recognised that historic assets that are subject to those forces will not be considered at risk if they are subject to a planned programme of managed change (for further details see Dunkley 2008).

Preservation by investigation (usually known as 'preservation by record') can be applied when preservation *in situ* is not practicable. This practice often comprises survey, excavation, recording, recovery of archaeological remains, analysis, archiving, and publication (for details on each of these activities please refer to Chapter 3). It also presents challenges within the marine environment, which are further discussed in the following section.

Management is based on the assessment of risk and vulnerability (see Dunkley 2008). Effective management requires reliable data on which to base preservation and conservation priorities. To achieve this, a variety of different methodological and technical approaches to quantifying the marine cultural resource have been undertaken. Quantification of the resource needs to be tailored to its needs:

assessment of the known and potential record, as well as quantification of the potential threats (both natural and anthropic) to the resource, is needed. Management of the marine cultural resource also involves engagement with industries operating in the marine environment, with development consultation, and with regulators and the planning and consents process. Within this context, strategic and methodological projects have been commissioned to allow informed decisions on the management process. At a strategic level English Heritage has set up tangible protection outcomes for management purposes which are outlined in the National Heritage Protection Plan (NHPP).[5] Recently, especially through initiatives such as the Aggregates Levy Sustainability Fund (ALSF) (Section 4.6), awareness about the finite and non-renewable nature of the cultural resource has been raised within government and offshore industries. The ALSF has made a substantial contribution to emerging public policy in respect of the marine historic environment. Archaeological projects funded through the ALSF have provided strategic, methodological, and practical tools for industry and contributed to reduce directly the impact of aggregate extraction on the marine historic environment. More importantly, ALSF work shows the relevance of this resource for all sectors of society and demonstrates that effective collaboration between industry, curators, archaeological contractors, researchers, trusts, and societies is possible and beneficial, contributing to a sustainable management of the historic environment for present and future generations (see Dellino-Musgrave 2007; Dellino-Musgrave *et al* 2009; Flatman & Doeser 2010). The ALSF has therefore provided a proactive, rather than reactive, model of innovative heritage management, where public and private sectors collaborate in the strategic management of the marine historic environment. Unfortunately, the UK government decided to discontinue the ALSF from the end of March 2011. However, there is currently lobbying from the industry and environmental partners to reinstate it as a means of supporting marine spatial planning and the UK marine science strategy (Ed Salter pers comm March 2011) (further details on the UK marine science strategy are provided in Chapter 4).

Finally, some independent groups, such as the Joint Nautical Archaeology Policy Committee (JNAPC), the CBA, and the IfA Maritime Affairs Group, address broader issues related to the profession as a whole which contribute to advances in the practice of maritime archaeology. They promote professional standards for present and future generations' management, conservation, understanding, and enjoyment of the maritime archaeological resource.

2.2.3 Development-led work

Archaeological projects undertaken within a development-led context arise from development consent processes within offshore developments (details are provided in Chapter 3). Through the development consent process, planning and development applications are referred to curators who will provide advice aimed at ensuring the preservation of the marine historic environment. These planning and development applications relate to both large-scale (eg offshore wind farms, port developments

Figure 2.5 The number of offshore renewable energy developments has increased dramatically in recent years, with an associated increase in related development-led archaeological assessments (Image courtesy of English Heritage)

such as London Gateway, the aggregate industry, and oil and gas) and small-scale (eg additional pontoons to marinas, new slipways, and oyster farms) projects. To take one example, offshore wind energy is expected to provide a large portion of the UK's renewable energy in the future (Fig 2.5). Therefore, applications for offshore wind farms have increased, especially with recent announcements (2009–10) of the round two and round three wind farm development areas.[6] In Ireland, the proposed locations for these wind farms are mainly on the offshore sandbanks, which are areas of high underwater archaeological potential. Sandbanks are natural shipping hazards and, as such, have been a focus of wrecking throughout history. When reviewing these applications, recommendations of detailed underwater archaeological assessments of the area to be impacted are made. As sandbanks can cover large areas, geophysical surveys are generally requested, followed by ground truthing by archaeological divers of any identified anomalies with archaeological potential (see Kelleher 2007). This process is also taking place in other areas of the UK, with recommendations of archaeological assessments made through diving, remotely operated vehicle, and ground truthing in advance of development work. Where known archaeology is present, avoidance and preservation *in situ* are the preferred options.

The principle of preservation by investigation discussed in the previous section can also apply in development-led contexts. In the past few years several examples have arisen as a result of the maintenance and development of shipping channels. For example, the Princess Channel Wreck was found by the Port of London Authority as a result of the maintenance of shipping channels. This case raised issues of protection of historic assets within ports and harbours. The investigation and excavation of the wreck by an archaeological contractor took place and what remained of the vessel was recovered (Auer & Firth 2007; Ransley 2007). The ship's timbers were taken to Horsea Lake, near Portsmouth, where they provide an underwater training site for maritime archaeologists under the auspices of the NAS.

Development-led archaeology has enabled advances in our knowledge of different aspects of the marine historic environment. For example, military aircraft crash sites, which are an important part of Britain's military and aviation heritage, have been reported through schemes such as the BMAPA/English Heritage *Protocol for reporting finds of archaeological interest* (BMAPA & English Heritage 2005), which aims to reduce any adverse effects of marine aggregate dredging on the historic environment by enabling people working in the industry to report their finds in a manner that is convenient and effective. The Protocol has been designed to deal with discoveries made on the seabed, onboard, and at wharves. The Protocol's implementation service has enabled its successful introduction and widespread adoption, with the aim of providing an easy-to-use mechanism for reports to be made by industry staff. It also facilitates the transfer of details of finds, and subsequent data, to the National Record of the Historic Environment of England (NRHE of England) and appropriate local Historic Environment Records (HERs). From an archaeological perspective, the study of aircraft (with emphasis on military aircraft) within the marine context is a growing field. Thousands of aircraft are likely to have been lost in British waters during the 20th century, and many of these losses are likely to be combat or accidental losses of military aircraft during World War II, as is suggested by the records of aircraft crash sites (such as those available through the NRHE of England) and the role played by aviators during this time. The remains of an aircraft hitting the ground or the sea would vary depending on the type of construction and whether the aircraft was lost in combat or by accident (as a result of, for example, adverse weather conditions or malfunction). Aircraft crash sites are a tangible reminder of the extent of aerial activity over and around the UK during the two World Wars and further systematic studies are needed in the marine environment. In addition, such crash sites are often associated with loss of life (sometimes represented by *in situ* human remains), and as such they need to be respected because they provide a focus for commemoration and remembrance. The Protection of Military Remains Act (1986) provides protection to aircraft crash sites or ships deposited in UK waters since the outbreak of the First World War (see Chapter 4).

All archaeological work in the marine environment produces large amounts of undeposited archive material. Archives consist of paper, photograph, video, and drafting film records, along with samples and a wide range of objects that can be well preserved in the marine zone. Increasingly large numbers of digital files are being produced, particularly through development-led archaeology. These include geophysical survey data sets, photographs, video, GIS files, databases, and reports. For example, geophysical surveys are a requirement for offshore wind farms to enable, among other things, the assessment of the impact of these developments on the historic environment. These surveys also have the potential to increase knowledge about the historic environment interest of an area. Therefore, the security and availability of marine archaeological archives is crucial in allowing further research, education, and amenity initiatives, providing the opportunity for beneficial cumulative knowledge regarding marine archaeology (further discussed in Chapter 3).

Marine archives are an important resource for which it is often difficult to find long-term repositories. These archives have traditionally fallen outside the remit of either terrestrial or maritime archaeological museums. A large volume of archive is currently undeposited and held by the various sectors previously mentioned (HWTMA 2009a; 2009b; 2009c). Within the archaeological contractors sector, which has mostly undertaken work in a development-led framework, there are currently few instances where the deposition of data in an accessible archive is specifically included within conditions of consent or permissions for work, and there are few resources to monitor whether this has been achieved. Hence, the application of best practice is often not achieved. The Archaeological Data Service (ADS) OASIS (Online AccesS to the Index of archaeological investigationS) system is designed to provide a record of archaeological 'events' which at least provides an indication of work undertaken. OASIS is beginning to be more regularly utilised in the marine zone, and recently the following condition has been included on any new dredging permission granted by the Marine Management Organisation (MMO):

> An OASIS form is to be submitted for any archaeological reports produced as part of this DP [dredging permission] and a copy submitted to English Heritage Maritime Archaeology Team and a PDF file version sent to English Heritage's National Monuments Record (oasis@english-heritage.org.uk). The operator should notify to English Heritage if they have directed an appointed consultant to complete this requirement.
>
> (Ed Salter pers comm, March 2011)

2.2.4 Education and outreach

The majority of sectors involved in marine archaeology have an education and outreach (E&O) element to their remit. E&O activities can take many forms, from public dissemination via the internet through public engagement events and projects to bespoke educational programmes and resources.

Truly inclusive E&O programmes aim to reach the broadest possible audience in terms of age and background. This can be achieved through programmes

Figure 2.6 The HWTMA Maritime Bus at a community day in Gosport, Hampshire (Image courtesy of HWTMA)

within formal education systems, such as school assemblies/workshops, learning outside the classroom sessions, or the provision of curriculum-linked resources.[7] Outreach programmes aimed at the wider general public typically operate beyond 'traditional' formal educational systems and establishments and can include public exhibitions or community-based projects. For example, the HWTMA's Maritime Bus takes maritime archaeology into the heart of communities, thereby helping overcome access barriers (Fig 2.6).[8]

Means of educating and engaging the public are many and varied, from information leaflets and posters through popular and educational publications, presentations, exhibitions, and resources to public events, activities, and projects.[9] Funding for marine archaeology education and outreach activities is often obtained through programmes and supporters whose primary concern is public engagement and learning, rather than heritage or the marine historic environment.

In an educational context, the main challenge is the constraint of an intense and prescriptive National Curriculum (particularly at secondary school level) in which archaeology is considered to be a very minor component of the history curriculum and both marine archaeology and the cross-curricular nature of the subject are largely unrecognised. The 'playing field' is also subject to change, with successive governments indicating their intention to restructure the form and content of the National Curriculum.

Outreach programmes must overcome the fact that the marine archaeological resource and activities are often out of sight and inaccessible to the general public. This perception can be compounded in non-coastal communities, as people often assume that marine archaeology concerns only shipwrecks off the coast and therefore has little relevance to them.

2.3   Current challenges

This section discusses the main challenges that the marine archaeology sector is currently facing.

There is a limited knowledge of the marine cultural resource, mainly as a result of its location, nature, and extent. For example, knowledge of the continental shelf climate and environment is mostly derived from terrestrial (eg pollen) or marine (eg deep sea core) records (Ransley *et al* forthcoming, Chapter 1). Evidence from the continental shelf itself focuses primarily on geomorphology, such as the organisation of fluvial systems substantiated through the analysis of submerged palaeovalleys (eg Gupta *et al* 2007; 2004). However, there are still issues of chronology and correlation to be addressed, especially owing to the fragmented nature of offshore deposits and the limited range of radiocarbon dating. There are also large gaps in knowledge related to offshore environments, especially in the Irish Sea, which is subject to less work than the English Channel and North Sea (Ransley *et al* forthcoming, Chapter 1).

Locating and recording submerged prehistoric landscapes is also challenging since baseline data is still needed to aid the characterisation of exposed palaeo-landsurfaces and enable cross-cultural comparisons to be made in order to understand past settlement and migration patterns in context (Bell & Warren forthcoming). It has been recognised that drowned landscapes between continents hold the key to understanding past human dispersal into Europe, the Americas and Australasia. To overlook this issue is to discount a fundamental part of the human story by providing an incomplete and biased record (Bailey 2004; Erlandson 2001). Consequently, this information is essential to the study of past human evolution, migration, and global dispersal. It is also central to defining this cultural resource and addressing issues of its long-term management.

The discussion above has highlighted the limited integration of different scales of analysis when seeking an understanding of the past. There is a need to integrate these scales of analysis further in order to allow a more comprehensive understanding of the past. For example, the studies of ships need to be integrated with our knowledge of vessel technology, life on board, shipbuilding yards, and the social and material networks within which these aspects were set. The technological milestones in vessel construction need to be better understood and contextualised with the social realities of the period under study. There is significant potential in expanding the analysis of vessels beyond technical and military issues by addressing the complex web of socio-political factors which shaped them.

There is a need to continue gathering reliable and accessible data to enable effective management of the marine cultural resource. Such data are used to help shape policy. Policy development is evidence-based, and new knowledge should thus be reflected within it (HM Government et al 2010). The marine archaeological community therefore needs evidence-based information to continue to lobby for legislative change and to develop legislation and management that properly serves the interests of the marine archaeological resource.

For reasons beyond the scope of this book, marine archaeology has produced, and is still producing, archives that are not being deposited in public repositories and hence made secure and accessible (for further details see HWTMA 2009a; 2009b; 2009c; Ransley et al forthcoming). A number of simple actions, including awareness-raising through publications and training and the distribution of (and adherence to) existing standards and guidance, could rectify this situation. More broadly, there is a requirement for the establishment of proper archive facilities, such as a museum or archive resource centre. Without such a centre it will remain virtually impossible (or at least extremely difficult) to implement the deposition of archives. If archives of past, present, and future marine archaeological investigations are not made publicly available, their future cannot be secured for present and future generations.

2.4 Summary

This chapter has briefly discussed the key areas and issues that are faced by different sectors involved in marine archaeology. Going beyond availability of funds, the key challenges presently faced can be summarised as follows:

- limited knowledge of the marine cultural resource, mainly related to its location, nature and extent;
- limited integration of different scales of analysis, currently preventing a more comprehensive understanding of the past;
- a need for reliable and accessible baseline data to enable effective management of the marine cultural resource;
- archives from investigations are not being deposited in public repositories and hence are largely inaccessible;
- a need to change the perception that the marine archaeological resource and its investigation are out of sight and therefore inaccessible to the public.

To summarise: archaeology is, if nothing else, about new ideas concerning the past (Johnson 2000, 9). Whether undertaken by professional or voluntary practitioners, marine archaeological work inherently involves ongoing challenges and debates, and this will remain the case. It is through these challenges and debates that the archaeological discipline grows as a whole.

Endnotes

1   See www.soton.ac.uk/archaeology/research/projects/maritime_research_framework.html.
2   See www.socantscot.org/scarf.asp?Menu.
3   See www.archaeoleg.org.uk/.
4   See www.science.ulster.ac.uk/cma/.
5   See www.english-heritage.org.uk/professional/protection/national-heritage-protection-plan/.
6   See www.thecrownestate.co.uk.
7   eg www.hwtma.org.uk/schools www.maryrose.org/learning/index.html; www.wessexarch.co.uk/learning/schools.html.
8   See www.hwtma.org.uk/maritimebus.
9   In addition to the organisation cited above, see www.nauticalarchaeologysociety.org.

CHAPTER 3

Marine archaeology projects

This chapter presents some of the basic steps that professional archaeologists follow on marine projects. In general terms, it is important to note that in the marine environment there are two main types of projects: research and development-led. Research projects can cover any type of archaeological research from, for example, submerged prehistoric landscapes to shipwreck and aircraft remains. They tend to be focused on a particular site or area in order to address a specific research objective. These objectives are often part of a long-term research process or over-riding research framework (Section 2.2). By contrast, development-led archaeological projects usually occur as a component of pre-disturbance assessment work undertaken in association with commercial developments in the marine and coastal zone. Consequently, there is no real pattern to the type or nature of sites that development-led projects investigate, and the sampling strategy is determined by the patterns of development itself. Despite this difference, both types of project can contribute to the understanding of the past that we develop from the results of the analysis and interpretation of archaeological remains.

In general, and for clarification purposes, archaeological projects follow some basic steps:

- project planning
- desk-based research (ie collection and assessment of available data)
- fieldwork (data collection)
- assessment for future analysis
- analysis and interpretation
- report preparation and publication
- dissemination
- archiving

3.1 Project planning

Any archaeological project starts with questions which are formalised in a research or project design. The project design sets out the work that is going to be undertaken (ie questions expressed in aims and objectives), how it is planned to carry it out (ie methods to be used to answer the questions), and why (ie the contribution the project is expected to make to wider understanding) (for further details see Gamble 2001). The project design will also include details of the scope, duration, and costs of the work. English Heritage has formalised the project planning process through its guidance *Management of Research Projects in the Historic Environment* (*MoRPHE*) (for further details see English Heritage 2006b).

Together with the development of the 'ideas' underpinning the proposed research, the following aspects can be considered as part of the design process:

- desk-based study: this involves the collation and assessment of existing documentary sources and previous archaeological work in the project area to understand the current state of knowledge. Consideration of who else is currently engaged in work that may have implications for the proposed research is also useful at this stage;
- permits: initial enquiries to obtain an idea of whether the proposed research would require permits;
- funding: a consideration of the cost implications of the project and from where the potential sources of funding could be obtained;
- resources: if funding is obtained, the right people to do the work will need to be in place with time available to undertake work within the proposed timescale;
- impact on people, organisations, and legislative and planning authorities: a consideration of who could be affected by the proposed work during short, medium, and long timescales. Liaison with the relevant people, organisations, and authorities in advance helps to demonstrate the feasibility of the proposed work.

In the UK, for development-led projects, developers, port authorities, and others proposing to dredge or undertake any development work in the marine environment go through a procedure which includes the submission of an Environmental Impact Assessment (EIA) before consent to undertake development is granted (Section 4.6), whereby the environmental effects of a development project may be assessed (DCLG 2000; 2006). The Marine Management Organisation (formerly known as the Marine and Fisheries Agency) administers a range of statutory controls that apply to marine works, including all construction, coastal defences, dredging, and the disposal of waste materials at sea in waters around the UK (which is done on behalf of the Secretary of State for Environment, Food and Rural Affairs). Consents for the majority of development work usually require some form of marine archaeological assessment to be undertaken and may involve subsequent work to mitigate against the impacts of the proposed development on the marine historic environment. Consequently, the involvement of an archaeological consultant or contractor to identify and then undertake appropriate assessment and highlight potential mitigation requirements at an early stage of development proposals is often a cost-effective strategy.

All persons on the investigating team must be suitably qualified and experienced for their project roles. All investigations underwater should be undertaken only under the direction and control of a named maritime archaeologist with recognised qualifications and experience appropriate to the investigation. The IfA is the professional organisation for archaeologists in the United Kingdom, and advances the practice of archaeology and allied disciplines by promoting professional standards and ethics for conserving, managing, understanding, and promoting the enjoyment of heritage. Registered Organisations (ROs) and archaeologists are admitted to corporate membership after rigorous peer review of their competence, experience, and qualifications. Consequently, using ROs in development-led contexts provides a measure of quality assurance as regards their competence. All ROs and members agree to abide by the IfA *Code of Conduct* (IfA 2010), thus adhering to the highest professional and ethical standards.[1]

3.2 Collection and assessment of available data

Any archaeological project should assess the existing corpus of work to understand the current state of knowledge as well as to enable the identification of gaps. Obtaining a comprehensive understanding of the known and potential heritage assets for a given study area (or comparable examples from other areas) in order to enable informed assessments and aid future management decisions is also important. This is often referred to in the sector as the gathering of baseline data. Baseline data can vary considerably in quality and coverage. This is because the purposes for gathering such baseline data differ (eg the data requirements for assessing the geomorphology of an area are different to those required from an archaeological perspective). Hence, it is important to consider how representative of past activities those data are by understanding and assessing the available data sources, how and why those data have been gathered, and their applicability for heritage assessments.

The gathering of baseline data is often undertaken during the production of a desk-based assessment (DBA). This is an assessment of the known and potential heritage assets within a specified site or area. It consists of a collation of existing documentary, graphic, photographic, and electronic information aimed at identifying the likely character, nature, extent, and quality of the known or potential heritage assets in a local, regional, national, or international context, as appropriate (IfA 2001). The assessment may lead to one or more of the following:

+ the formulation of a strategy to ensure the recording, preservation, or management of the resource;
+ the formulation of a strategy for further investigation, whether or not intrusive, where the character and value of the resource is not sufficiently defined to permit a mitigation strategy or other response to be devised;
+ the formulation of a proposal for further archaeological investigation within a programme of research.

Within development-led contexts, DBAs are often produced as part of an EIA. EIA procedures have been determined by a European Council Directive (85/337/EEC as amended) which came into force in 1988. The main aim of the Directive is to ensure that the authority giving the primary consent for a particular project makes its decision with full consideration of any probable significant effects on the natural and historic environment (DCLG 2000; 2006). In order to achieve this a DBA must utilise information about the construction and operation of the proposal in order to consider the development's impact upon the marine historic environment. It will also consider the significance of the effects of any such impacts, taking into account previous disturbance and the importance of the known and potential marine historic environment. It must also outline recommendations for mitigating significant adverse effects on the marine historic environment and identify any residual effects – defined as effects that will occur notwithstanding mitigation and the need for further work where applicable (for further information see BMAPA & English Heritage 2003; JNAPC 2008; Wessex Archaeology 2007). Further details on legislation and management contexts are provided in Chapters 4 and 5.

The methodology adopted for the assessment will need to reflect best practice in undertaking archaeological desk-based assessments as outlined by the IfA's *Standard and Guidance for Archaeological Desk-based Assessment* (2001), the BMAPA and English Heritage's *Marine aggregate dredging and the historic environment: guidance note* (2003),[2] Wessex Archaeology's *Historic Environment Guidance for the Offshore Renewable Energy Sector* (2007),[3] and the JNAPC's *Code of Practice for Seabed Development* (JNAPC 2008).[4]

Especially within a development-led context, geophysical surveys may have been undertaken for a variety of physical and environmental assessments, and the results are often reviewed at the DBA stage. As per survey data, it is crucial to review any geophysical data and identify features of potential archaeological significance alongside an archaeological DBA. This will allow data analysis, comparison, and interpretation as well as provide contextual information of the study area, following the recommended best practice which has already been outlined within this section.

Discussed below are the main organisations and sources suggested for consideration within a DBA of baseline information in the marine historic environment. A description is provided following a very brief summary of how they could be useful from a marine archaeology perspective.

3.2.1   National records

Briefly, national records are very useful because, among other things, they provide:

- a starting point in the quantification and identification of national historic environment records;
- information on archaeological and architectural remains, maritime wrecks, casualties (documented losses), and aircraft, among other things;
- an initial idea of patterns resulting from the use of the seas.

3.2.1.i   England

In England, during the 1990s the Royal Commission on the Historical Monuments (RCHME, since merged with English Heritage) initiated the recording of sites and structures of archaeological and historic interest in England's Territorial Waters to complement its existing record of terrestrial sites. An ongoing process of research and recording continues today and has been fully integrated as part of English Heritage's National Record of the Historic Environment (NRHE). The NRHE contains nearly 400,000 records and is accessible online via the PastScape website.[5]

3.2.1.ii Scotland

The Royal Commission for the Ancient and Historical Monuments of Scotland (RCAHMS) was originally founded in 1908 and renewed in 2000. The RCAHMS collects, records, and interprets information on the architectural, industrial, archaeological, and maritime heritage of Scotland. Its archive offers a unique insight into the special nature of Scotland's historic assets and the records are also searchable online (see Chapter 4). The RCAHMS is specifically charged with extending its record to offshore areas.[6]

3.2.1.iii Wales

The Royal Commission for the Ancient and Historical Monuments of Wales (RCAHMW) was originally founded in 1908 and renewed in 2000. The RCAHMW has a leading national role in developing and promoting understanding of the archaeological, built, and maritime heritage of Wales as the originator, curator, and supplier of authoritative information for individual, corporate, and governmental decision-makers, researchers, and the general public. The RCAHMW holds a unique collection of photographs, maps, images, publications, and reports within its archive, the NMR of Wales, which can be consulted via the online database Coflein. The RCAHMW is charged with the task of extending the Welsh NMR to offshore areas. Also available is the Core Archaeological Record Index (CARN), a national information resource for archaeology and architecture compiled by archaeological organisations across Wales.[7]

3.2.1.iv Northern Ireland

In Northern Ireland, the Centre for Maritime Archaeology (University of Ulster) holds a wreck database which has recently been updated, separating records compiled from the United Kingdom Hydrographic Office (UKHO) database from sport divers' reports. There is also an online database for shipwrecks which has been compiled by sport divers.[8] Coastal and intertidal sites are included within the Northern Ireland Sites and Monuments Record, which can be accessed online via the Northern Ireland Environment Agency website.[9] Currently, there is not a centralised database for submerged prehistoric landscapes. However, there is some information available online for intertidal peat sites at the Northern Ireland Earth Science Conservation Review webpage.[10] Although useful, this information is primarily geological and biological rather than archaeological.[11]

3.2.2   Historic Environment Records/Sites and Monuments Records

Local authorities are responsible for maintaining a register of all the known archaeological sites in their area. These databases are known either as Historic Environment Records (HERs) or as Sites and Monuments Records (SMRs) (or in some historic towns as Urban Archaeological Databases (UADs)).

In England, some HERs are available online and can be accessed through the Heritage Gateway.[12] In Scotland, the HER records are available via the online Highlands Historic Environment Record database.[13] 'Historic Wales' is a map-enabled portal for historic environment information. The portal allows simultaneous searching of hundreds of thousands of records relating to archaeological monuments, historic buildings, and artefacts held by different organisations across Wales, including information from the Welsh HERs and Cadw.[14] 'Built Heritage' maintains the Northern Ireland SMR for the six counties of Northern Ireland, holding information on around 15,000 sites. This database, and more information on Northern Ireland's SMR, is available from the Monuments and Buildings Record.[15] Search facilities are also available via the ADS.[16]

The name 'Historic Environment Record' has been adopted by many authorities to reflect more closely the increasing breadth of information which they record about the historic environment. HERs/SMRs are the major source of information for understanding the local historic environment (including coastal and intertidal zones) for all site types and periods. The inclusion of a site on an HER/SMR gives it formal recognition in the planning process, and local planning authorities take account of this in drawing up development plans and reaching planning decisions. These records are maintained and updated for public benefit as a valuable research and educational resource. They also inform management policies. While they were initially developed to provide advice through the planning system, HER/SMRs are now used extensively for sustainable management and conservation of the historic environment.

3.2.3   UK Hydrographic Office

The United Kingdom Hydrographic Office (UKHO) is primarily concerned with the gathering and supplying of data for navigational safety purposes. It has been responsible for charting wrecks since 1913, and has a history of marine survey dating back for centuries. All known wrecks around the British Isles are held in a database maintained by the UKHO Wreck Information Service.

The UKHO records are organised within four main categories:

+ ABEY: A previously reported wreck but not detected by survey, leading to doubts about its reported position or existence
+ DEAD: A wreck not detected by repeated surveys, therefore considered not to exist
+ LIFT: A salvaged wreck
+ LIVE: All other wrecks, charted or uncharted

The UKHO is also the national archive for hydrographic material and holds an extensive collection of historic charts and other material, such as printed and manuscript navigational surveys and charts dating from the 17th century; printed and manuscript sailing directions, coastal views, and ships' remark books from about 1750; printed books and atlases relating to the history of maritime cartography and exploration; and record copies of Hydrographic Department publications from about 1830.

Data supplied by the UKHO can be useful to provide:
- information about the use of the seas;
- information about the distribution of vessels;
- tools to allow a more comprehensive understanding of vessels within their natural environment;
- through maps, charts and plans, an idea of the existing knowledge of certain areas as well as offering the means to evaluate them further.

3.2.4   The Receiver of Wreck

Since 1993 the Receiver of Wreck (RoW) has been centralised, dealing with all reports of wreck from around the UK. It is based within the Maritime and Coastguard Agency (MCA) headquarters in Southampton and has assistance from Coastguard personnel around the coast. The RoW can provide useful information mainly about specific wrecks, their finds, and, in some cases, ownership. Further information on the RoW and its role is provided in Chapter 4.2.

3.2.5   Ministry of Defence

Within the remit of this handbook, it is relevant to mention the role of the Ministry of Defence (MOD) Salvage and Marine Operations team, which supports the Armed Forces and other government departments within marine projects. The team is responsible for the salvage of any ship, submarine, aircraft, or other military equipment as required by the Armed Forces. It also salvages civilian aircraft. The Salvage and Marine Operations team manages any MOD-owned shipwrecks that pose a risk to the environment. Other relevant areas of the MOD are the Naval Historical Branch, Naval Heritage, RAF Heritage, and Joint Casualty and Compassionate Centre. These can provide information about, among other things, military vessels, historic records, and casualties.[17]

3.2.6   Local record offices, museums, and libraries

Local record offices, museums, and libraries can provide further information in the form of various documentary sources and artefacts recovered by trawlers or divers. For example, collections of artefacts from trawlers or divers have often been recovered unsystematically. Although they would not necessarily be considered a formal 'archive', they can provide an idea of the archaeological potential of the seabed.

These sources can offer, among many other things:

- detailed information about a site or an area;
- detailed information about climate changes, challenges faced at sea, sailing routes, etc;
- information about purpose of journeys, possible intermediate stops, cargo lists and characteristics, diet on board, etc;
- information about people and events in a certain period;
- shipping arrivals and departures.

These sources often hold archaeological archives from past investigations as well as a host of other specific information. Although these should be consulted, it should be borne in mind that, owing to the long-term lack of coordination of archive deposition, and the fact that these institutions do not have a specific responsibility to collect maritime archaeology archive material, the usefulness of these archives in a particular area cannot be guaranteed. In general terms, the further offshore the research or development is, the smaller the amount of relevant information that is held within coastal record offices. However, some coastal museums or exhibitions (whether public or private) could also hold relevant material. There is an online catalogue of maritime and naval museums in Britain and Ireland which lists around 300 museums and museum-ships in Britain and Ireland, providing contact details and opening hours.[18]

3.2.7 Bathymetric, geotechnical, and geophysical data

Bathymetric (water depth), geotechnical (stratigraphic and sediment) and geophysical (generally gathered to analyse potential petroleum reservoirs and mineral and soil deposits, to locate groundwater, to locate archaeological finds, and for environmental remediation) survey data are gathered in both commercial and research contexts. The information generated from these types of data can be interpreted in many ways. For example, data interpretations relating to times of lower sea level can provide an understanding of potential areas of landscape used by human populations in the past that are now submerged.

Owing to the varying contexts in which these data are collected, the specifications and quality of the data can also vary considerably. From an archaeological perspective, this variability in specifications and quality affects the contribution the data can make to archaeological interpretations. Depending on the quality, these data can help to provide an understanding of broader regional changes or even enable a more detailed assessment of (known and potential) archaeological features on the seabed.

3.2.8 Secondary sources

There are numerous secondary sources that can be considered during DBAs. For example, the 'diver' series of guides to known sites can provide clarification on thte position, form, and identity of some wrecks. Information related to maritime archaeological research, sea level, and coastal change can be gathered from various academic journals, books, and monographs. There is also a wealth of 'grey literature' – a term often used to describe unpublished material such as internal reports. This type of material can be very difficult to trace but initiatives such as 'ALSF online' make unpublished reports freely accessible online.[19]

In general, there is an overall lack of clarity over specific roles and responsibilities related to curation and enforcement of conditions of consent and deposition of archives within the marine zone. Although development-led archaeological reports should be logged with either the local authority HER officer or the NMR, this does not always occur. However, some work is underway through OASIS.[20]

In addition, the British Geological Survey Offshore Regional Reports series and accompanying maps describe the offshore geology of the UK and complement the regional geology guides which cover the onshore areas. These allow interpretation to facilitate the assessment of the potential for derived and *in situ* prehistoric archaeological material within geological contexts related to the Pleistocene and early Holocene epochs. These British Geological Survey publications also illustrate 'in-fill' and more recent surface sediments that can provide information on the potential environments of more recent heritage assets.

3.3   Fieldwork

After the collection and assessment of the available data, fieldwork might be deemed appropriate or necessary. The different stages of practical work that can take place, depending on the aims and objectives of the proposed work, are summarised as follows:

+ pre-disturbance survey
+ monitoring survey
+ evaluation/excavation
+ site stabilisation

These stages of practical work will need to follow some minimum requirements and recording standards as stated in the Standards and Guidance produced by the IfA.[21]

The pre-disturbance survey covers a wide variety of non-intrusive archaeological investigations, such as:

+ performing geophysical surveys
+ undertaking photography and video
+ compiling site plans
+ recording seabed topography
+ measuring and drawing objects on the seabed

Further detailed information on these methods can be found in Bowens 2008. As indicated by its name, pre-disturbance survey work should not in any way disturb the site or area being surveyed. Often, the archive generated will be deposited within the relevant heritage body, such as English Heritage, Historic

Scotland, Cadw, or the Environment and Heritage Service (Northern Ireland). Depending on the funds available, archiving can also take place via the ADS.

Monitoring, as the name implies, observes how a site or an area changes through time (Bowens 2008). Monitoring can take place in different ways, such as:

- geophysical surveys: depending on the available funding, these could provide comparable data, allowing any changes across an area or site to be identified and monitored. The viability of a geophysical approach to site monitoring has been demonstrated through recent work along the south coast of England (eg Bates *et al* 2011; Plets *et al* 2007);

- installation of monitoring points around a site: this would allow measurements to be made between the points and the surrounding seabed. Their comparison over time should provide a picture of the relative accumulation/erosion of sediment around the site. An ongoing example of this is provided by the monitoring of the site of HMS *Colossus* on the Isles of Scilly (Camidge 2009);

- diver observations: these would allow the production of updated site plans which could be compared to previous diving seasons. These would aid in the identification of elements that are still visible, and those that are no longer visible or have degraded away. This type of work has been conducted on the site of the French warship *La Surveillante* (Breen *et al* 2001).

Evaluation/excavation involves the exposure, processing, and recording of archaeological remains (for further details see Bowens 2008). For example, in the UK any activity which involves disturbance of a designated site requires an excavation licence. This licence will not normally be issued until a completed pre-disturbance survey and project design have been submitted to the relevant heritage agency. In most cases, the direction of such activities would have to be under the control of an archaeologist with the appropriate expertise.[22]

The purpose of site stabilisation is to ensure the stability of a site on the seabed to maximise its preservation. Different site stabilisation methods have been tested on the Swash Channel (Palma & Parham 2009) and HMS *Colossus* (Camidge 2009) protected wreck sites (Fig 3.1). The purpose of this strategy is usually to encourage the build-up of sediment across the site, effectively reburying a shipwreck that has become exposed as a result of previous sediment movement.

Figure 3.1 Artificial sea grass deployed as one of the stabilisation methods on the early 17th-century Swash Channel shipwreck. The remains of the vessel are one of the UK's designated protected shipwrecks (Image courtesy of Paola Palma, Bournemouth University)

This can greatly reduce the effects of erosion and destructive marine organisms on any exposed wooden timbers and artefacts.

As a result of the activities described above a fieldwork archive will be generated in which the following should be recorded: name and location of site or area visited; type of activities undertaken; and materials recovered (if applicable). The fieldwork archive should be quantified, ordered, and indexed. A review of the quality, character, and significance of the data collected can then be undertaken and an assessment of the potential for analysis could be performed if considered pertinent. In other words, the fieldwork archive from a marine archaeological investigation should be subject to the same standards as those from terrestrial investigations (Ransley *et al* forthcoming).

3.3.1   Health and safety for diving projects

The health and safety of the investigating team and any third parties is a prime concern in a diving project. A 'diving project' is the term used for the overall diving job, regardless of the time taken or the number of diving operations necessary (HSE 1998). A diving operation shall be identified in the diving project plan. It can be composed of either a number of dives or even a single dive and can be safely supervised by one supervisor (HSE 1998).

All persons on the investigating team must work according to a safety policy that satisfies both relevant statutory and professional requirements, which come under the Diving Operations at Work Act 1997, irrespective of the conditions and methodology. When directing a project, employers have a duty of care to participants and the main aim must be safety. Since 1998, when these regulations came into force, the Health and Safety Executive has produced a set of 'Approved Code of Practice' (ACoP) for each sector of the commercial diving industry, one being for scientific and archaeological diving projects (see HSE 1998). However, this is only a general template. Projects of any significant scope will need to develop a site-specific code of practice to cover all eventualities. It is common, therefore, that archaeological organisations have a code for diving operations and archaeological projects. In addition to this, supplementary measures/rules will usually be added to the code to take account of site-specific circumstances and potential hazards. Therefore, safety documentation comprises three tiers: 1) HSE ACoP; 2) Archaeological Organisation code; 3) Site-specific appendix. Further information on diving at work is available from the HSE website.[23]

In the UK, contact with the appropriate authorities to advise them of the proposed work will need to be made where there are health and safety implications. They may request CVs of all team members, copies of their diving certificates and medicals, and copies of all certification for plant and equipment. If the project is being undertaken under the auspices of a museum or university, their relationship with the health and safety authorities may already cater for such circumstances.

As part of health and safety measures a risk assessment is also needed for archaeological diving projects. The risk assessment is an official document in which possible risks are systematically identified in each stage of the project. Each identified hazard must be matched by a mitigating measure. For example, when diving, a particular hazard could be presented by working with a compressor, owing to high noise levels. A procedure to eliminate this hazard would be the wearing of ear-protectors by compressor operators at all times. Risk assessments have to be written for every project and a copy filed with the organisation's safety officer.

Recreational diving organisations such as the BSAC and the Sub-Aqua Association (SAA) have published guidance on safe diving practices, while BSAC Technical Services provides guidance on risk assessment for diving. This specific guidance places emphasis on the prevention of incidents and promotes safe diving practices to all divers. Furthermore, all diving should adhere to the Combined Diving Associations' *Respect our Wrecks* initiative by following the Code of Practice for Wreck Divers.[24]

The MCA is responsible for navigational and ship operation matters and carries out health and safety enforcement on ships and boats.[25] Accidents on ships and boats should be reported to the Marine Accident Investigation Branch, which may investigate them and publish findings and recommendations with a view to preventing their reoccurrence.[26] Regarding vessel safety, the Combined Diving Associations have produced *Guidelines for the Safe Operation of Member Club Dive Boats*.[27] Small Vessels operating commercially under the British flag or in British waters must comply with the Merchant Shipping Regulations or an MCA Code of Practice. At sea, a vessel's Master has overall responsibility for the safety of the vessel and everyone on board. It is everyone's duty to comply with any instructions issued by the Master.

3.4 Assessment for future analysis

In general terms, the purpose of an assessment for future analysis is to evaluate the potential of the data from a site or area (eg records, samples, and artefacts, among other things) that could contribute to further archaeological knowledge and identify future areas of study. Different types of data and material will, of course, require different methods of assessment. The assessment can help in establishing the potential of the integrated data to shape further research questions and inform decisions about future analysis and interpretations.

For example, the Bournemouth University project 'Mapping Navigational Hazards as Areas of Maritime Archaeological Potential', funded by English Heritage through the ALSF, aimed to identify and characterise areas where a high risk of ship losses coincides with a high potential for preservation. Areas of Maritime Archaeological Potential (AMAPs) are areas where a high risk of ship losses caused by the presence of navigational and environmental hazards coincides with a high potential for preservation where seabed conditions are favourable to the preservation of archaeological materials (Merritt *et al* 2007). The project used

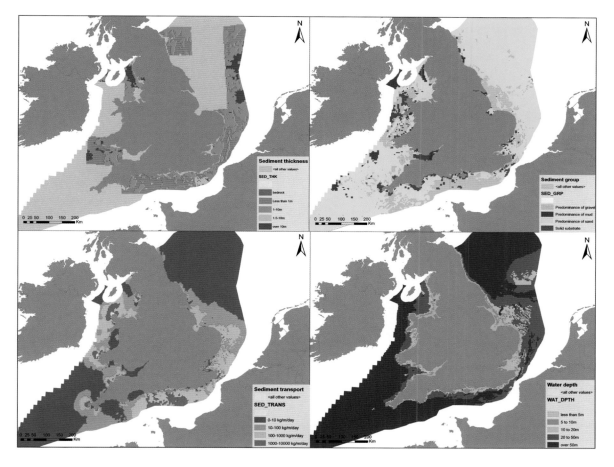

Figure 3.2 AMAP2 environmental characterisation vector grid, symbolised by sediment thickness, sediment group, sediment transport, and water depth. The grid is derived from UKHO and BGS datasets (Image courtesy of Olivia Merritt, SeaZone Solutions Ltd, and English Heritage)

varied data sources (eg UK hydrographical archives and modern seabed geology mapping) to identify and map AMAPs. It highlighted the scope for making better use of available wreck data and identified the need to integrate a broad range of environmental variables into the analysis, providing the foundations for two further phases of work to characterise AMAPs. The project 'AMAP 2 – characterising the potential for shipwrecks' is currently testing and building on the results of AMAP 1, 'Refining areas of maritime archaeological potential for shipwrecks'. Funding for both these projects was obtained from the ALSF and distributed by English Heritage (Merritt 2008; 2010). The current AMAP 2 project, completed in 2011, used statistical and spatial analysis of shipwreck data to enable a comparison of typologised wreck scatters with environmental, historical, and hydrographic datasets using a GIS platform in order to contextualise areas previously identified as AMAPs across a trial area during AMAP 1 (Fig 3.2) (Merritt 2008; 2010; 2011).

The HWTMA *Flower of Ugie* project is another example which demonstrates the broad nature of projects undertaken. Work on the wreck of the *Flower of Ugie* (referred to until the identification of the vessel as the 'Mystery Wreck') began as part of the HWTMA's Eastern Solent Marine Archaeology Project in 2004. This

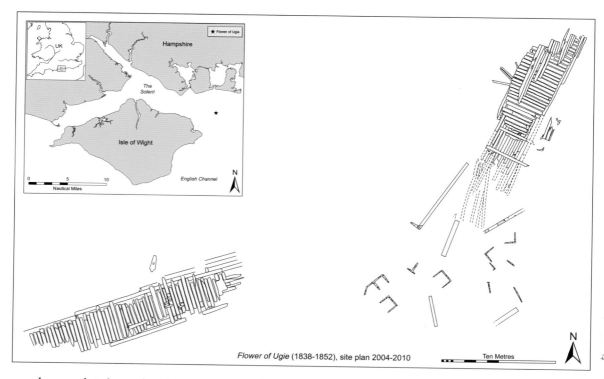

Flower of Ugie (1838-1852), site plan 2004-2010

Ten Metres

wooden wreck is located within an aggregate licence area off Horsetail Sands in the Eastern Solent. Diving work undertaken by the HWTMA between 2004 and 2008 had revealed a site split into two large sections (Fig 3.3). At the time survey-recovered artefacts and samples indicated a possible late 18th-century or early to mid-19th-century wreck. Owing to the urgent need to investigate the date and identity of the vessel to help determine its archaeological significance and to develop sustainable long-term monitoring and management of the site, funding from the ALSF, distributed by English Heritage, was awarded for this project in 2009. An initial DBA was undertaken utilising the current site archive, in addition to the gathering of a wide range of historic and environmental data related to the site and the surrounding area. Collaboration with United Marine Dredging, a division of Tarmac Ltd, resulted in a review of their available geophysical data from the area and provision of their detailed knowledge of the Eastern Solent. This work was further enhanced through specialist assessment of wood samples and metal artefacts. The results were used to prioritise fieldwork for the 2009 diving season, which included the completion of survey work on the eastern and central sections, further timber and artefact sampling, and the establishment of monitoring points on site. In 2010 further research and analysis involved specialist review of artefacts and documentary research at a range of archives. Continuing work was undertaken on the monitoring of the site as described within this section, through both the measuring of installed monitoring points and diver observations of the surviving wreck structure. The results of the DBA, fieldwork, artefact and material analysis, historical research, and site monitoring are now being published and disseminated (Whitewright & Satchell 2011).[28]

Figure 3.3 Location and site plan of the *Flower of Ugie* (1852) in the Eastern Solent. See also Figs 1.5 and 2.4 (Image courtesy of HWTMA)

3.5 Analysis and interpretation

Archaeology can be defined as a social science that seeks to increase knowledge about people in the past through the study of the material remains that they left behind. Therefore, archaeological questions are necessary so that sensible answers, or even more questions, can be generated (Gamble 2001). To achieve this, using time and space as a framework, systematic methods and approaches are followed which lead to subsequent analysis and interpretations (see Gamble 2001). Consequently, the analysis of information, artefacts, samples, and, ideally, the full site archive gathered as part of the methods and approaches applied will take place. Where applicable, key areas can also be developed for further specialist analysis. This information is then holistically interpreted to enable a more comprehensive understanding of a site or area. Social, economic, political, and technological contexts are also considered through historical and archive research, and comparison with other sites or areas may be carried out. Analysis and interpretation will naturally lead to preparation of a report or publication in an academic monograph or journals.

Holistic approaches of analysis and interpretation are exemplified in the work undertaken on the site of Bouldnor Cliff, situated off the north coast of the Isle of Wight, which has produced some of the most intriguing Mesolithic artefacts from Britain to date (see Chapter 2; and for further details refer to Momber 2000; 2004; 2006; Momber *et al* 2009; 2011; Tomalin 2000). The characteristics, nature, and extent of the site have been researched and the unique levels of preservation resulting from its waterlogged nature have facilitated a series of specialist analyses (eg wood identification, dendrochronological dating, and environmental analysis). For example, the woodworking techniques identified (Fig 3.4) are not otherwise seen in Britain until 2000 years later, at the Neolithic site of Haddenham (see Evans & Hodder 2006). These techniques show high levels of social organisation, possibly with the intention of creating a large structure, and may imply a level of sedentism, or at least repeated visits to specific areas of the landscape (see Momber *et al* 2011). Alternatively, the same techniques have been linked to the creation of log boats and, given the site's proximity to water, this could be an interesting

Figure 3.4 Worked tree trunk from the site of Bouldnor Cliff. A branch of the tree has been torn off and the splintered wood trimmed, leaving distinctive marks in the surface of the timber (Image courtesy of HWTMA)

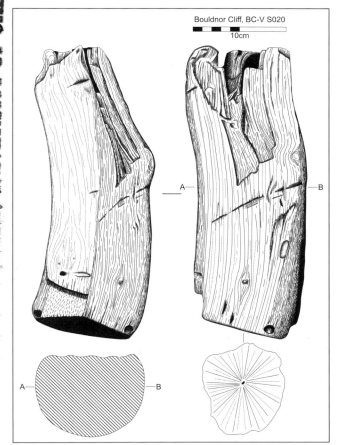

Bouldnor Cliff, BC-V S020

10cm

interpretation. This was supported by the flint specialist analysis, which also offered an understanding of the surrounding terrestrial archaeology that would have been roughly contemporary with Bouldnor Cliff. These links between 'terrestrial' and 'submerged' environments have been crucial when dealing with Mesolithic hunter-gatherer landscapes in order to understand fully the varied facets of the lives of Mesolithic people (for further details see Momber *et al* 2011; see examples in Chapter 2).

3.6 Report preparation and publication

Published research results are crucial to scientific development and make significant contributions to the archaeological discipline as a whole. The most common forms of archaeological publication are books, monograph series, journal articles, and academic reports. However, more publicly accessible publications, such as booklets and leaflets, allow a wide audience to be reached. This in turn contributes to raising awareness and promotes a more comprehensive understanding of our common past.

Within an academic context the publishing process has been formalised within UK higher education through the Research Assessment Exercise (RAE), first undertaken in 1986. The RAE introduced a formal assessment process of the quality of research.[29]

Other types of reporting could involve the result of those projects funded by heritage organisations or those which have been produced as a result of a development-led project. Some of these reports end up as unpublished reports or 'grey literature', which can often be found through the relevant funding bodies (eg English Heritage, Historic Scotland, Cadw, or the Environment and Heritage Service (Northern Ireland)) or through online initiatives such as ALSF online.[30]

3.7 Dissemination

Communicating the past to others is one of the main responsibilities of archaeologists. Britain's history, as noted in Chapter 2, is inextricably linked to its surrounding seas. To realise the value of this unique heritage for stakeholders and the wider community, it is important to promote the 'heritage cycle' (Fig 3.5) (English Heritage 2005), through which an increasing understanding of the historic environment leads to people valuing it more and as a consequence caring for it better. An environment that is cared for may be more easily enjoyed, and enjoyment normally brings a thirst to learn more. Therefore, it is through wide dissemination of project results that increased knowledge of, and improved access to, our maritime past can be achieved.[31]

Figure 3.5
The Heritage Cycle
(Image courtesy of
English Heritage)

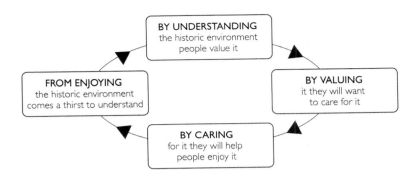

BY UNDERSTANDING
the historic environment
people value it

FROM ENJOYING
the historic environment
comes a thirst to understand

BY VALUING
it they will want
to care for it

BY CARING
for it they will help
people enjoy it

3.8   Archiving

The completion of any archaeological project, whether research-focused or related to development work, should be the deposition of the full archive within a public museum or repository. Archives from the marine zone are subject to the same standards as those generated by terrestrial investigations. Best practice in relation to archaeological archives has been outlined by Brown (2007), who examines the archiving process, including creation, compilation, transfer, and curation. All elements of an archive are included within this process, whether documentary, drawn, photographic, samples, digital, or objects. All elements should be deposited together and made publicly accessible. However, it should be noted that, particularly within England but also beyond territorial waters, the fate of maritime archaeological archives is not always clear, as there are few museums willing or able to access and curate maritime archives.[32] To help address this situation it is important that long-term planning for archives is considered from the project planning stage, and that the relevant heritage agency is approached for advice if there are difficulties in identifying a suitable museum or repository (Fig 3.6).

Figure 3.6 Archiving the material developed through research and fieldwork into the warship *Hazardous* (Image courtesy of HWTMA)

3.9   Summary

This chapter presented some of the basic steps that professional archaeologists follow within research and development-led projects. Although the scope of archaeological projects varies considerably, they should always be undertaken following archaeological standards and best practice. Whether in land or maritime contexts, the significance of archaeology remains the same: enhancing the understanding of our common past and communicating this information to the community.

Endnotes

1   See www.archaeologists.net.
2   www.bmapa.org/downloads/arch_guidance.pdf.
3   www.offshorewindfarms.co.uk/Pages/Publications/Archive/Cultural_Heritage/
     Historic_environment_g43354590/.
4   www.jnapc.org.uk/publications.htm.
5   For more information visit www.pastscape.org.uk/default.aspx.
6   See www.rcahms.gov.uk/index.html and www.jura.rcahms.gov.uk/PASTMAP/
     start.jsp.
7   For more information visit www.coflein.gov.uk/, www.rcahmw.org.uk/ and
     www.rcahmw.gov.uk/HI/ENG/Search+Records/CARN/.
8   See www.irishwrecksonline.net/.
9   www.ni-environment.gov.uk/other-index/content-databases/content-databases-
     ambit.htm.
10   www.habitas.org.uk/escr/.
11   For more information visit www.science.ulster.ac.uk/esri/Centre-for-Maritime-
     Archaeology,65.html#page=introduction.
12   www.heritagegateway.org.uk/Gateway/CHR/.
13   www.her.highland.gov.uk/.
14   www.jura.rcahms.gov.uk/NMW/start.jsp.
15   www.ni-environment.gov.uk/built/mbr/mbr.shtml.
16   www.ads.ahds.ac.uk/catalogue/.
17   www.mod.uk/DefenceInternet/Home/.
18   www.people.pwf.cam.ac.uk/mhe1000/marmus.htm.
19   www.ads.ahds.ac.uk/project/alsf/.
20   See www.oasis.ac.uk/.
21   For further details visit www.archaeologists.net/.
22   For further details see www.english-heritage.org.uk/maritime.
23   www.hse.gov.uk/diving.
24   www.bsac.com.
25   www.mcga.gov.uk/.
26   www.maib.gov.uk/home/index.cfm.
27   www.bdsg.org/14866%20SS%20Guidelines.pdf.
28   www.hwtma.org.uk/flower-of-ugie.
29   www.rae.ac.uk/
30   www.ads.ahds.ac.uk/project/alsf/.
31   For examples on dissemination initiatives please see www.hwtma.org.uk and
     www.nauticalarchaeologysociety.org.
32   For further information see 'Securing a Future for Maritime Archaeological
     Archives' project www.hwtma.org.uk/maritime-archaeological-archives.

CHAPTER 4

Current UK marine administration, policy, and legal context

This chapter sets out basic information regarding the administration, formal policy, and legal context relating to the protection and management of underwater cultural heritage within the UK. Thus far only specific components of the whole range of legislative and management tools have been addressed in an overtly maritime context (Dromgoole 2006; Williams *et al* 2005). The main aim of this chapter is therefore to provide a first port of call for those requiring wider general guidance on this subject. In most cases direction to further, often more detailed, sources is included.

UK legislation relating to shipwrecks dates back to the 19th century. However, it is only since the 1970s that legislation has been concerned specifically with maritime 'heritage', rather than simply salvage law. The history of the development of this legal protection is outlined in Section 4.3. Since 1997, the process of administrative devolution undergone by the UK has complicated the way in which maritime heritage is protected and managed. The often labyrinthine system of parliamentary acts and planning policies is not always uniformly applied across the constituent countries of the UK. The ongoing devolution process is likely to lead to the further fragmentation of this system in the coming years. It is already the case that maritime heritage is protected and managed differently in some parts of the UK than in others. The complexity of the situation has been further increased since the turn of the century as a result of attempts to bring the management and protection of maritime heritage into line with that of terrestrial heritage. This process has witnessed the publication of major policy statements by agencies such as English Heritage (Roberts & Trow 2002), setting out their vision of how this integration should be achieved. Although this process is still ongoing, this chapter represents a first attempt to summarise the entire current situation within a single document.

The chapter is subdivided into a number of sections that guide the reader through several different subjects and topics. These encompass: stakeholders and users; organisations responsible for maritime heritage; UK maritime legislation; and planning and development control for coastal and marine zones. Additionally, a section on 'guidance and resources' provides information about where many of the documents, policies, guidance notes, and so on can be accessed. The legislation, policies, and guidance documents that are covered in this chapter will inevitably change over time. However, the agencies of legislative and policy change tend to remain the same. Accordingly, an emphasis has been placed on providing direct links to such sources/institutions/organisations that will be responsible for any future alterations and amendments.

The huge scope of the material that is covered within the limited confines of this chapter dictates that coverage of individual elements may sometimes seem cursory. No apology is made for this: it is simply a necessity of fitting a large subject area into the confines of this book, the focus of which is very much on the wider discipline of maritime archaeology.

4.1 Stakeholders and users

Stakeholders and users include the general public as taxpayers but also all those interested parties involved with the coastal, intertidal, and marine zones. These include, among others, BMAPA companies and other UK aggregate producers, the Seabed User and Developer Group, Collaborative Offshore Wind Research Into The Environment (COWRIE), The Crown Estate, the National Trust, port and harbour authorities, sports diving organisations (eg PADI, BSAC, SAA) and members of the public engaged in activities such as fishing, sailing, pleasure boating, and walking.

4.2 Organisations responsible for maritime heritage management

Within the UK a number of different organisations and institutions have responsibility for heritage management and consultation. Many of those that have responsibility for terrestrial affairs also have a remit for maritime heritage. Additionally, there are a number of organisations/institutions that have a purely maritime remit. These bodies range from UK-wide governmental departments through devolved heritage bodies to special interest advisory groups. The basic remits and roles of this wide variety of organisations, institutions, civil servants, and individual citizens in relation to maritime heritage in the UK are described in Section 4.2. Despite the range of organisations/institutions that are concerned with heritage protection there are still elements of maritime heritage that fall outside these roles or remits. Areas of responsibility are constantly evolving, in conjunction with the ongoing development of accompanying legislation.

4.2.1 UK-wide governmental departments and bodies

4.2.1.i Department for Culture, Media and Sport

The Department for Culture, Media and Sport (DCMS) is the UK government department responsible for policy relating to a wide range activities, including the historic environment. The Secretary of State for Culture, Olympics, Media and Sport is responsible for the listing of historic buildings and scheduling of ancient monuments in England on the basis of specialist advice provided by English Heritage (see Section 4.2.2.i). The Secretary of State is also responsible for wreck designation in UK territorial waters adjacent to England and Northern Ireland on the basis of advice received from the heritage bodies situated in those countries. This designation responsibility has been devolved to Scottish and Northern Irish ministers and the Welsh Assembly government. Anyone can apply to the Secretary of State for a wreck to be designated under the Protection of Wrecks Act 1973 (see Section 4.3.1).[1]

4.2.1.ii The Receiver of Wreck

The Receiver of Wreck (RoW) administers cases of voluntary salvage of wreck material across the whole of the UK related to the Merchant Shipping Act (Section 4.3). Its aim is to ensure that the interests of both the salvor and the owner are considered. Its remit covers UK territorial waters as well as wreck landed in the UK from outside these waters; it extends to tidal waters, but does not cover lakes. The RoW is based within the headquarters of the Maritime and Coastguard Agency, in Southampton.[2]

The advent of sports diving has led to an increasing focus on the salvage of underwater cultural heritage. Consequently the RoW takes an active role through liaison with partner organisations (eg the NAS, the JNAPC) and through education schemes aimed at the diving community.

4.2.2 UK national heritage bodies

4.2.2.i English Heritage

English Heritage was established in 1984 and is the government's statutory advisor on the historic environment within England.[3] English Heritage (English Heritage 2005, aims) has six stated aims:

- to help people develop their understanding of the historic environment;
- to place the historic environment on other people's agendas;
- to enable and promote sustainable change to England's historic environment;
- to help local communities to care for their historic environment;
- to stimulate and harness enthusiasm for England's historic environment;
- to make the most effective use of the assets in our care.

Within this remit English Heritage has the responsibility of assisting the Secretary of State in the listing of historic buildings and scheduling of historic sites and monuments of national importance, as noted above. English Heritage is also responsible for maintaining the List and the Schedule. English Heritage involvement relating to development control is generally limited to cases or schemes involving designated assets or where there is significant impact on the historic environment. However, English Heritage also advises the government regulators the MMO on the implications of marine developments on the marine historic environment. Under the National Heritage Act 2002 (see Section 4.3.1), English Heritage provides advice and recommendations to the UK government relating to the marine historic environment in UK territorial waters adjacent to England. English Heritage receives public funding through DCMS and DEFRA and generates other income from its historic sites and related activity.

4.2.2.ii Historic Scotland

Historic Scotland (HS) was formed in 1991 and is now an executive agency of the Scottish Government.[4] The aims of Historic Scotland (2008, 1.3) are threefold:
- to care for, protect and enhance the historic environment;
- to secure greater economic benefits from the historic environment;
- to help people value, understand, and enjoy the historic environment.

HS advises Scottish ministers on all aspects of the historic environment within Scotland. It is also responsible on behalf of Scottish ministers for administering devolved heritage protection legislation such as the scheduling of monuments of national importance, the listing of historic buildings, and the designation and licensing of wreck sites in UK territorial waters adjacent to Scotland under section 1 of the Protection of Wrecks Act 1973. HS is funded by the Scottish Government and obtains additional income from historic properties and related activities.

4.2.2.iii Cadw

Cadw (the Welsh word meaning 'to keep') is the historic environment service of the Welsh Assembly government.[5] In relation to the historic environment of Wales, Cadw aims to:
- protect and sustain;
- encourage community engagement;
- improve access.

Cadw is responsible for the scheduling of historic sites and monuments of national importance and for listing historic buildings. Under the National Heritage Act 2002 (see Section 4.3.1), Cadw has responsibility for making decisions relating to the designation and licensing of wreck sites in UK territorial waters adjacent to Wales. Cadw also advises the Welsh Assembly government regarding the conditions imposed by the licensing of offshore development. Cadw is funded by the Welsh Assembly government.

4.2.2.iv Northern Ireland Environment Agency

The Northern Ireland Environment Agency (NIEA) is part of the Department of Environment within the Northern Ireland government (DOENI).[6] Within the NIEA the Built Heritage Directorate has responsibility for the management of the historic environment, including the protection of monuments and maintaining the Northern Ireland Sites and Monuments Record (NISMR). Maritime heritage is not included within the NISMR, being contained instead within a separate Maritime Record which is maintained in partnership with the Centre for Maritime Archaeology at the University of Ulster, Coleraine. Under the National Heritage Act 2002 (see Section 4.3.1), DOENI has responsibility for advising DCMS regarding the designation and licensing of wreck sites in UK territorial waters adjacent to Northern Ireland.

4.2.3   Other institutions and groups

4.2.3.i Advisory Committee on Historic Wreck Sites

The Advisory Committee on Historic Wreck Sites (ACHWS) was the advisory non-departmental public body sponsored by DCMS to advise government on the suitability of wreck sites for designation and licensing under the Protection of Wrecks Act 1973. Abolished in March 2011, the Committee's responsibilities have been devolved to the national agencies described above which either now have, or are in the process of creating, new national advisory bodies for designation and licensing under the 1973 Act (see below 4.3.1.i).

4.2.3.ii Joint Nautical Archaeology Policy Committee

The Joint Nautical Archaeology Policy Committee (JNAPC) was formed in 1988 and comprises individuals and institutional representatives who wish to raise awareness of the UK's underwater cultural heritage.[7] Their stated aim is to persuade the UK government that such heritage should receive protection equal to that of terrestrial sites. The JNAPC has played an important role in the consultation exercises that have accompanied much of the recent and ongoing heritage reform relating to the marine historic environment. The JNAPC continues to recommend that the UK Government should ratify the UNESCO Convention on the Protection of Underwater Cultural Heritage (JNAPC 2010).

4.2.3.iii Institute for Archaeologists

The Institute for Archaeologists (IfA) is an independent professional organisation for archaeologists and those who work in the historic environment.[8] It represents the interests of archaeologists to government, policy-makers, and industry. The IfA also aims to advance the practice of archaeology and allied disciplines through the promotion of professional standards and ethics. The IfA has a special interest group relating to maritime archaeology, the Maritime Affairs Group, which provides a forum for practising maritime archaeologists and advises the IfA Council on issues relevant to maritime archaeology. The Maritime Affairs Group aims to promote the advancement of maritime archaeological practice and the greater understanding of maritime archaeology within the wider archaeological community. It also promotes professional standards for the management, conservation, understanding, and enjoyment of the maritime archaeological resource; aids in the development of professional guidelines and standards for the execution of maritime archaeological work; promotes the training of archaeologists and others in maritime archaeological practice; and facilitates the exchange of information and ideas about maritime archaeological practice and communicates these to the wider profession.

4.2.3.iv Nautical Archaeology Society

The Nautical Archaeology Society (NAS) is an independent, non-governmental organisation formed with the intention of furthering interest in underwater cultural heritage.[9] As such, the NAS is dedicated to advancing education in nautical archaeology at all levels. The main vehicle for achieving this is the NAS training programme, which operates throughout the UK and provides an introduction and ongoing training in all aspects of maritime archaeology. The NAS is also responsible for publishing the *International Journal of Nautical Archaeology*.

4.3 Legislation

In 2002 English Heritage published a policy statement on the management of maritime archaeology in England, expressing its view that 'The current legislative and planning regime for marine archaeology in England is out of date and does not adequately permit the adoption of approaches and standards that are regarded as routine in terrestrial heritage management' (Roberts & Trow 2002, 16). It is worth briefly considering how a maritime nation such as the UK reached this undesirable position.

Legislative provision for the protection of shipwrecks (and material from shipwrecks) within UK waters dates back to the late 19th century (Merchant Shipping Act). However, this was primarily concerned with establishing ownership of salvaged material, rather than with the dedicated protection of underwater cultural heritage. The first legislation specifically aimed at underwater heritage protection (Protection of Wrecks Act) was not enacted until the 1970s and was concerned only with the application of archaeological standards when salvaging shipwrecks in order to prevent activity that could be perceived as 'looting'. Other underwater site-types, such as submerged landscapes, remained unprotected. This situation was exacerbated when national legislation to protect broader archaeological sites was introduced in 1979 (Ancient Monuments and Archaeological Areas Act), but was not actively extended to archaeological remains below the low-water mark. A further layer of legislation was introduced in 1985 to furnish protection to naval war graves resulting from the World Wars (Protection of Military Remains Act). By the end of the 20th century the UK still maintained a set of legislation that treated terrestrial and underwater archaeology in different ways. Additionally, the emphasis on *in situ* preservation and ongoing sustainability that has become a central theme of modern heritage management remained absent from the management of underwater cultural heritage within the UK.

It is against this background that organisations such as the NAS and the JNAPC have lobbied to improve the protection granted to the UK's maritime heritage. The first decade of the 21st century has witnessed the initiation, but not the completion, of this process. For example, the remit of the UK's heritage agencies has been extended into the UK's territorial waters. However, devolution of legislative powers has added a further layer of complexity as the devolved administrations of the UK are able to formulate their own nationally specific and distinctive legislation. Although it must be hoped that the development and introduction of legislation will proceed at an even pace across the UK, it is already becoming clear that this will not be the case. In particular, the extended powers granted to the Scottish parliament have facilitated the faster reform of heritage legislation in that country than in the other areas of the UK. It could be reasonably stated that, at the time of writing, underwater cultural heritage is better protected in the UK territorial waters off Scotland than in those of England, Wales, and Northern Ireland. The primary legislation currently in force, along with the major pieces of draft legislation which may comprise part of the legislative framework in the future, are summarised below.

4.3.1   Legislation relating to UK marine cultural heritage

The following section summarises the principal pieces of legislation that relate to underwater cultural heritage within the UK. This account is by no means exhaustive and should serve only to familiarise the reader with the legislation that they are likely to encounter. In some respects, the legislation relating to the protection and management of underwater cultural heritage is gradually coming into line with that for terrestrial heritage. However, the failure of the proposed Heritage Protection Bill to be enacted in England and Wales in 2009 has stalled any further progress for the time being. Fuller accounts of some of the earlier acts, including commentary on the relative effectiveness of the UK's maritime heritage legislation, can be found in Dromgoole 2006.

4.3.1.i The Protection of Wrecks Act (1973)

Applies to: UK

The Protection of Wrecks Act (PWA) was introduced as a means to prevent looting of shipwrecks deemed to be of historical interest. Although not originally intended to be a long-term tool for heritage protection, the PWA has remained the main piece of legislation for protecting underwater cultural heritage in the UK since its inception.

Shipwrecks deemed to be of historical, archaeological, or artistic importance can be designated by reference to a restricted area. In England, designation is

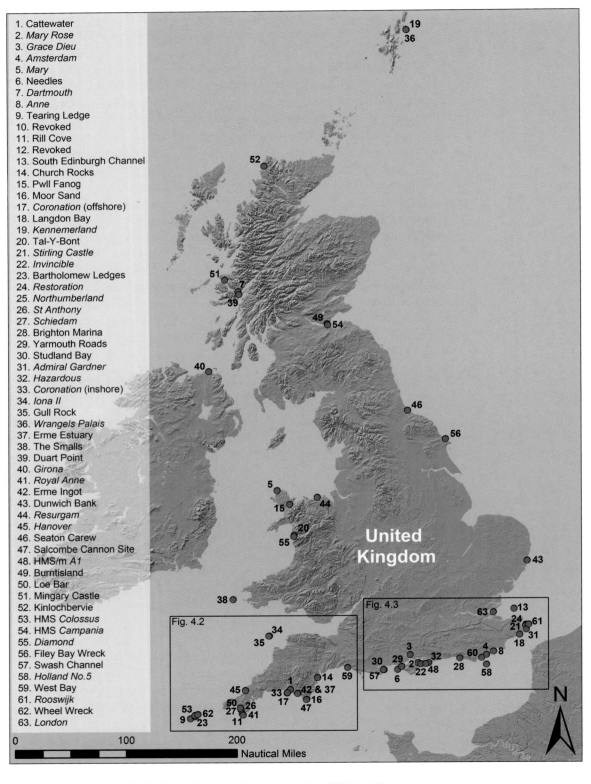

1. Cattewater
2. *Mary Rose*
3. *Grace Dieu*
4. *Amsterdam*
5. *Mary*
6. Needles
7. *Dartmouth*
8. *Anne*
9. Tearing Ledge
10. Revoked
11. Rill Cove
12. Revoked
13. South Edinburgh Channel
14. Church Rocks
15. Pwll Fanog
16. Moor Sand
17. *Coronation* (offshore)
18. Langdon Bay
19. *Kennemerland*
20. Tal-Y-Bont
21. *Stirling Castle*
22. *Invincible*
23. Bartholomew Ledges
24. *Restoration*
25. *Northumberland*
26. *St Anthony*
27. *Schiedam*
28. Brighton Marina
29. Yarmouth Roads
30. Studland Bay
31. *Admiral Gardner*
32. *Hazardous*
33. *Coronation* (inshore)
34. *Iona II*
35. Gull Rock
36. *Wrangels Palais*
37. Erme Estuary
38. The Smalls
39. Duart Point
40. *Girona*
41. *Royal Anne*
42. Erme Ingot
43. Dunwich Bank
44. *Resurgam*
45. *Hanover*
46. Seaton Carew
47. Salcombe Cannon Site
48. HMS/m *A1*
49. Burntisland
50. Loe Bar
51. Mingary Castle
52. Kinlochbervie
53. HMS *Colossus*
54. HMS *Campania*
55. *Diamond*
56. Filey Bay Wreck
57. Swash Channel
58. *Holland No.5*
59. West Bay
61. *Rooswijk*
62. Wheel Wreck
63. *London*

United Kingdom

Fig. 4.2

Fig. 4.3

N

0   100   200
Nautical Miles

Figure 4.1 Location and distribution of shipwrecks designated for protection under the Protection of Wrecks Act. At the time of writing (2012) this amounted to 61 shipwrecks. For clarity, the south-west and south-east of England are shown in further detail in Figs 4.2 and 4.3 respectively (Image courtesy of HWTMA)

Figure 4.2 Location of designated shipwrecks off the south-west coast of England (Image courtesy of HWTMA)

undertaken by the Secretary of State for Culture, Olympics, Media and Sport. In Scotland, Wales, and Northern Ireland it is conducted by the Scottish ministers, the Welsh Assembly government, and Northern Irish ministers respectively. Once the site of a shipwreck is designated it is an offence to remove, tamper with, or damage any part of the vessel. Likewise, it is an offence to carry out any unauthorised diving or salvage operation on the site. Access to the site is therefore restricted. Following designation, future work is controlled through a mechanism of licenses granted to individuals deemed to be competent and properly equipped to investigate the site.

The PWA was originally administered by the DCMS and previous government departments. In 2002 administration passed to English Heritage on behalf of the Secretary of State for Culture, Olympics, Media and Sport, as a result of the passing of the National Heritage Act 2002 (see Section 4.3.1.vi). Designated sites are monitored by contracted qualified diving archaeologists, who may also be used to assess potential sites prior to designation. The decision-making process relating to designation of sites, revocation of designations, and the granting/revoking of licenses has been overseen by the ACHWS, which included representatives of the relevant heritage agencies (eg Cadw in Wales). Following the disbanding of the ACHWS in 2010, the UK's heritage agencies now offer advice separately, directly to DCMS. There are currently 61 designated shipwrecks in UK waters (ACHWS 2009), which are illustrated in Figs 4.1 to

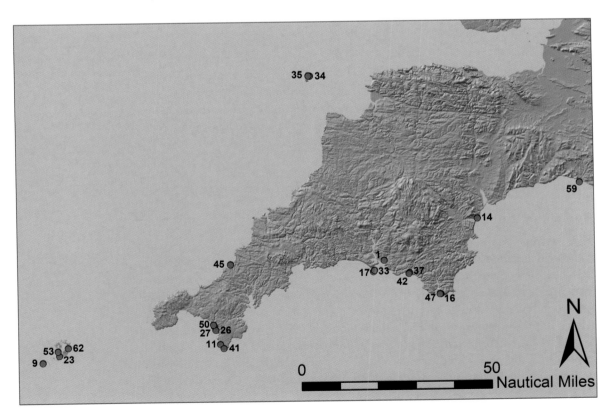

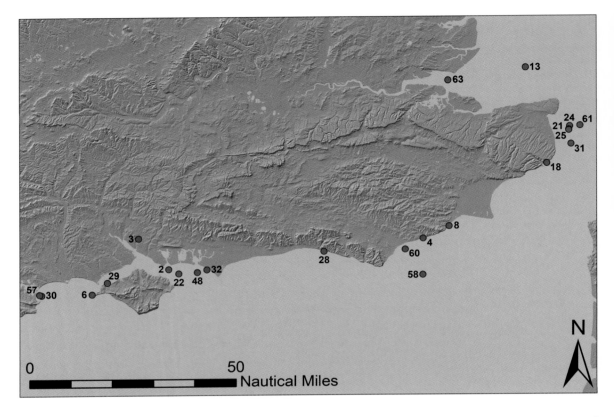

Figure 4.3 Location of designated shipwrecks off the south-east coast of England (Image courtesy of HWTMA)

4.3. Although the PWA allows for the strong protection of designated sites, it should be noted that designated vessels amount to only a tiny percentage of the total historic wreck assemblage that lies within UK territorial waters. The majority of the shipwreck resource therefore remains unprotected under legislation specifically concerned with maintaining the archaeological potential of such sites.

4.3.1.ii Ancient Monuments and Archaeological Areas Act (1979)

Applies to: England, Scotland, and Wales

The Ancient Monuments and Archaeological Areas Act (AMAAA) is the main legislation for the protection of ancient monuments. In Scotland, this has now been amended by the Historic Environment (Amendment) (Scotland) Act 2011 which introduces enhanced measures for protection. Although principally concerned with terrestrial heritage, the Act also allows for the protection of an ancient monument situated on or under the seabed within UK territorial waters. Monuments judged to be of 'national importance' may be added to the Schedule of protected sites and structures. Following scheduling it becomes an offence to demolish, destroy, alter, or repair a monument without consent. The designation of a scheduled ancient monument does not confer any rights or restrictions to access. Although the Act allows for the designation of Areas of Archaeological Importance, these are restricted to terrestrial concerns. Consequently, submerged landscapes or submerged areas of high archaeological potential have not currently been designated and it remains doubtful if a submerged landscape with no evidence of a 'structure' could ever be scheduled.

Several examples of scheduled maritime sites exist within the UK. Perhaps most notable are the seven remaining ships from the German High Seas Fleet that were scuttled at Scapa Flow, Orkney Isles, in 1919. These vessels have been scheduled by Historic Scotland in line with their policy of treating underwater remains in the same way as terrestrial remains. The AMAAA has been used to schedule the now-submerged remains of a field system off the Isles of Scilly, but as yet no vessel remains have been scheduled in English waters. English Heritage recently undertook a pilot study of a shipwreck site off the south coast of England, with a view to assessing the application of the AMAAA to such sites in the future.

All scheduled monuments are listed in a Schedule of Ancient Monuments maintained by the relevant heritage agency (eg English Heritage in England on behalf of the Secretary of State). The heritage agencies also advise the relevant government departments on new scheduling.

4.3.1.iii Protection of Military Remains Act (1986)

Applies to: UK

The Protection of Military Remains Act (PMRA) was passed with the objective of protecting the sites of aircraft or ships deposited in UK waters since the outbreak of World War One. The PMRA can cover Fleet Auxiliary and requisitioned vessels as well as those of purely military function, providing it can be demonstrated that a vessel was in military service at the time of loss. In addition, the PMRA also extends to cover the actions of British nationals or British vessels relating to those lost in international waters, but not in the territorial waters of another State. Vessels of a foreign State that lie in UK waters may also be covered. Aircraft or vessels can be designated as a 'protected place' or a 'controlled site' by the Secretary of State for Defence. The former may be visited, providing that no interference occurs; authorisation from the Secretary of State is required to visit the latter.

Following a consultation in 2001 a rolling programme of identification and assessment leading to designation was announced. The number of military vessels covered by the PMRA is therefore likely to increase over time. Ten vessels were added to the list in 2008, taking the total number designated, at home and abroad, to 58.

4.3.1.iv Historic Monuments and Archaeological Objects (Northern Ireland) Order (1995)

Applies to: Northern Ireland

The Historic Monuments and Archaeological Objects (Northern Ireland) Order (HMAO) allows for the protection of archaeological sites and objects within Northern Ireland and its territorial waters. This is carried out via a process of scheduling, in the same manner as provided for by the AMAAA. The HMAO also requires that anyone who discovers an archaeological object must report it within fourteen days.

4.3.1.v Merchant Shipping Act (1995)

Applies to: UK

The Merchant Shipping Act (MSA), which has its origins in the 19th century, was implemented in order to regulate the salvage of ships and their contents. The aim of the Act is to provide a means to deal with material resulting from the wreck or loss of ships, including the reuniting of material with its owners. The MSA applies to historic wrecks in the same way as more recent wrecks, but it does not apply to submerged landscapes or to the remains of human habitation and activity.

Finders of wreck (flotsam, jetsam, lagan, and derelict), including archaeological material, must declare their find to the Receiver of Wreck (RoW). The RoW will then publicise the recovered material so that it may be claimed. Any material remaining unclaimed after one year becomes the property of the Crown and the RoW may dispose of it. The nature of the MSA means that any material recovered during archaeological work on a shipwreck, whether or not it is designated or scheduled, must be declared to the RoW.

4.3.1.vi National Heritage Act (2002)

Applies to: England

The National Heritage Act (NHA) enabled English Heritage to assume responsibility for the management of maritime archaeology located within England's territorial waters. It extended the definition of an ancient monument, as set out in the AMAAA, to include heritage assets located in, on, or under the seabed within territorial waters. The concept behind this is that assets located underwater and within UK territorial waters should be treated in the same way as those located on dry land. The NHA also passed responsibility for the ongoing administration of the PWA from the DCMS to English Heritage on behalf of the Secretary of State. The NHA enables English Heritage to defray or contribute to the ongoing cost on managing those sites designated under the PWA.

4.3.1.vii Marine and Coastal Access Act (2009)

Applies to: England, Wales, Scotland, and Northern Ireland

The Marine and Coastal Access Act (MCAA) introduced a new framework for managing the marine resource of England and Wales, improving marine conservation, management of marine resources and extending public access to coastal areas. The objectives of the Act are delivered through the Marine Management Organisation (MMO). In conjunction with the Marine (Scotland) Act 2010 (see Section 4.3.1.viii), the MCAA provides a significant level of devolved responsibility to the constituent countries of the UK to manage their own marine affairs.

The MCAA has implications for maritime archaeology through the provision for coastal access, licensing of marine activities and controls over offshore development. However, provision for cultural heritage within the act is limited to reference to historic or archaeological matters that arise as a result of other considerations. For example, the establishment of a Marine Conservation Zone (MCZ) on the basis of an area's ecological and biological interest may also be beneficial for the preservation of historical or archaeological material lying within that zone. Similarly, restriction of certain types of fishing activity (eg beam trawling) can have added benefits for the protection of archaeological remains in the restricted area. The MCAA specifies (clause 54) that a number of issues must be kept under review by the relevant marine plan authority. These include the 'cultural characteristics' of the region and any considerations that might be expected to impact upon these. Cultural characteristics are specified (54(4)) as including those that are historic or archaeological in nature. Proposed partner legislation making provision for cultural heritage exists in the form of the draft Heritage Protection Bill (see 4.3.1.x), but this has yet to be passed into UK law.

4.3.1.viii Marine (Scotland) Act 2010

Applies to: Scotland

The Marine (Scotland) Act (M(S)A) is the Scottish counterpart to the MCAA that is in force in the other areas of the UK. Unlike the MCAA, the M(S)A also includes provision for the protection of the marine historic environment. This is in the form of designation of Historic Marine Protection Areas (MPAs) for the purpose of preserving a marine historic asset of national importance. The definition of a 'marine historic asset' is wide ranging and includes 'a deposit or artefact (whether or not formerly part of a cargo of a ship) or any other thing which evidences, or groups of things which evidence, previous human activity'. Such protection would replace any protection previously afforded under the PWA, of which section 1 is to be repealed in Scotland, once existing PWA-designated wrecks have been reviewed, and where appropriate, transferred to Historic MPA status.

Under the terms of the Act, a Historic MPA may extend from the sea to the area of related land adjacent to it and lying above the mean high water spring tide. This latter point may be seen as critical for providing a 'seamless approach' to heritage protection at the land/sea interface. Following designation it becomes an offence to intentionally or recklessly carry out any activity that damages, interferes with, or has a significant impact on the protected area. Similarly, it is an offence to intentionally or recklessly remove, alter, or disturb a marine historic asset within the protected area. Licenses may be granted to conduct activities (such as archaeological investigation) that might otherwise be considered an offence. The M(S)A received Royal Assent on 10 March 2010.

4.3.1.ix Historic Environment (Amendment) (Scotland) Act 2011

Applies to: Scotland

The Historic Environment (Amendment) (Scotland) Act 2011 amends three existing pieces of primary legislation: the Historic Buildings and Monuments Act (1953); the AMAAA; and the Planning (Listed Buildings and Conservation Areas) (Scotland) Act (1997). The Act addresses gaps and weaknesses in the existing legislation that were identified during a period of stakeholder consultation. The Act will harmonise historic environment legislation with the planning regime; improve the ability of central and local government in Scotland to work with developers and their partners; and improve capacity to deal with urgent threats and increase the efficiency and effectiveness of deterrents. The accompanying consultation document to the draft bill noted that protection for the marine historic environment was agreed as being no longer fit for purpose (Historic Scotland 2010, 12); however, it goes on to note that this was provided for in the M(S)A (see Section 4.3.1.v). It seems likely that, in the future, archaeology located wholly under water in the marine zone will normally be protected by the M(S)A while monuments on the foreshore, or with both landward and marine components, will be scheduled under the amended provisions introduced through the Historic Environment (Amendment) (Scotland) Act 2011. The level of protection extended by either Act is the same; for example, the revised definition of 'monument' also includes a 'site comprising any thing, or group of things, that evidences previous human activity' (Historic Environment (Amendment) (Scotland) Act 2011, Article 14). All the provisions of the Historic Environment (Amendment) (Scotland) Act were in force by late 2011.

4.3.1.x The Heritage Protection Bill (Draft)

Applies to: England and Wales

The aim of the draft Heritage Protection Bill published in 2008 was to establish a unified heritage protection system which simplified and harmonised the current separate systems of listing buildings, scheduling ancient monuments, designating

Scottish marine area (The Scottish Government 2010, 20) and a Scottish National Marine Plan is now in preparation. The marine planning system extends to the mean high water mark, while the terrestrial planning system extends to the mean low water mark. The need for these two systems to be complementary when dealing with the overlapping inter-tidal zone and the wider coastal zone is acknowledged in the SPP (The Scottish Government 2010, 20).

It is noted within the Scottish Historic Environment Policy that the historic dimensions of the Scottish environment may be found underwater as well as on land (Historic Scotland 2009, 5). With this in mind it is notable that within the SPP no separate mention is made of the marine historic environment, other than brief reference to preserving the integrity of scheduled or designated wreck sites (paragraph 119). It must be concluded on the basis of the SPP and Scottish Historic Environment Policy that the Scottish planning system sees no distinction, in terms of the protection afforded, between the terrestrial historic environment and the marine historic environment. The policies relating to the marine heritage resulting from the M(S)A have been integrated into the Scottish Historic Environment Policy in December 2011.

4.5.3 Planning: Northern Ireland

Within Northern Ireland, Planning Policy Statement 6 (PPS 6) represents policy relating to Archaeology and the Built Heritage. Published opinion (Williams 2001, 11) is that the same concepts for built heritage can be extended to the marine zone within the UK territorial waters adjacent to Northern Ireland. In April 2010 DOENI began the consultation process for a Northern Ireland Marine Bill. This bill is intended to oversee the management of areas of marine planning and development introduced within the MCAA (see Section 4.3.1.vii) which are specific to the waters of Northern Ireland. Within this document underwater cultural heritage is dealt with in only very general terms. It is acknowledged as being valuable, that protecting it is desirable, and that heritage bodies should be consulted when considering this (DOENI 2010, 3, 24, 29 and 34). It seems likely that the final policy will be along similar lines to that adopted in Scotland (DOENI 2010, 21).

4.5.4 Shoreline Management Plans

The Shoreline Management Plan (SMP) is an important tool for addressing coastal process, both natural and cultural, in England and Wales. It comprises a large-scale assessment of the risks associated with such processes, with the aim of reducing the identified risks to people and the developed, historic, and natural environment (DEFRA 2006, 4; Hansom *et al* 2004, 228). According to DEFRA (2006, 11), 'An SMP should provide the basis for policies for a length of coast and set the framework for managing risks along the coastline in the future.' The stated ideal is that the approach identified by the SMP will be applicable for the next 100 years (DEFRA 2006, 12). The first round of SMPs has been completed around the shores of England and Wales and these form the basis of current

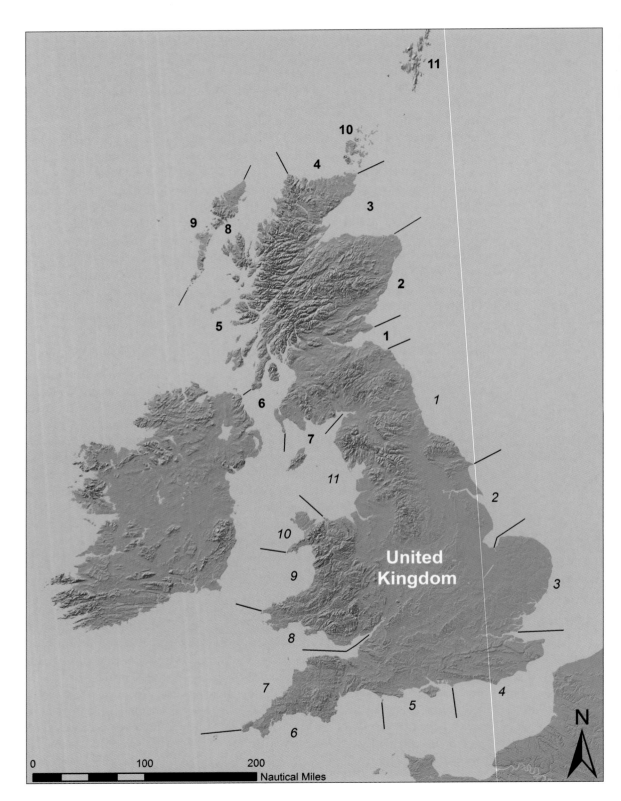

11

10

4

3

2

1

9

8

5

6

7

1

11

2

10

9

United Kingdom

3

8

7

5

4

6

N

| 0 | | 100 | | 200 | |
Nautical Miles

Figure 4.4
Geographic
distribution of
initial Shoreline
Management Plan
areas in the UK.
English and Welsh
zones are numbered
in italics; those
for Scotland are
numbered in bold
(Image courtesy of
HWTMA)

management policy in each particular area. These SMPs have been reviewed and a second generation of SMPs is being developed. Four SMP policies are available to shoreline managers (DEFRA 2006, 13–14):

- Hold the existing defence line: the maintenance or enhancement of existing coastal protection;
- Advance the existing defence line: the building of new defences on the seaward side of existing defences;
- Managed realignment: allowing the shoreline to alter in either a seaward or landward direction with management to control or limit such movement;
- No active intervention: there is no investment in coastal defences and natural processes are allowed to run their course.

Eleven broad SMP areas have been identified for England and Wales (Fig 4.4); these are, in turn, subdivided into a series of 'policy units' – simply a length of shoreline with similar characteristics in terms of coastal process and assets (DEFRA 2006, 41) and where sediment movement is relatively self-contained (Hansom *et al* 2004, 228–9). The similarity of the coastline within the policy unit means that a single policy (of the four available) can be applied. Of the available options, the latter two (managed realignment or no active intervention) are the most likely to result in impacts upon the historic environment. Selection of the preferred option relies upon a considered programme of consultation. English Heritage participates in this process in England in order to maintain the profile of the historic environment within such discussions. English Heritage's policy and approach to SMPs is outlined in *Shoreline Management Plan Review and the Historic Environment: English Heritage Guidance* (Murphy 2006). Further information about English Heritage's involvement in the SMP process can be sought from the Coastal Strategy Officer in the Maritime Archaeology Team at English Heritage.

It remains unclear if the notion of SMPs are as suited to the Scottish coast as they are to the coastline of England and Wales, mainly owing to the lower level of coastal development and also a lower level of coastal erosion (Hansom *et al* 2004, 231). Despite the lack of a statutory requirement for SMPs to be conducted in Scotland, the Scottish coast has been divided into a series of seven coastal cells (Hansom *et al* 2004, fig 1), since expanded to eleven (Fig 4.4), that form the basis of current/future SMPs.

4.5.5 Rapid Coastal Zone Assessment Surveys

Rapid Coastal Zone Assessment Surveys (RCZASs) were implemented by English Heritage in response to a lack of knowledge relating to the coastal historic environment (Murphy & Trow 2005, 8). RCZASs should provide an appraisal of the potential, significance, and vulnerability of coastal historic assets found in each policy unit identified in the SMP. This information can then contribute directly to SMP policy development (Murphy 2006, 3). A similar program of coastal surveys has been launched by the heritage agencies in the other constituent countries of the UK (eg Moore & Wilson 2006), with the same broad aim of expanding the knowledge base relating to coastal/intertidal heritage. These are often referred to as Coastal Zone Assessment Surveys (CZASs). Within England, the areas most under threat from coastal erosion and landscape change have been surveyed first.

RCZASs generally have two phases. Phase One comprises a DBA of data derived from sources such as aerial photographs, historic maps, the NRHE and local authority HERs. Phase Two consists of a walk-over survey that is designed to ground-truth the features of the historic environment identified in Phase One. Phase Two should also serve to locate and characterise any sites or features that are not visible in the data sources used in the Phase One assessment. The significance and vulnerability of all sites should also be assessed at this stage. Outputs derived from RCZAS should serve to enhance local authority HERs and the NMR. In addition, aspects of the results should be publicly disseminated (eg Hegarty & Newsome 2007; Paddenberg & Hession 2008). The RCZASs/CZASs that have been completed thus far have led to a large increase in the number of documented archaeological/historic sites located within the coastal zone. This should in turn lead to the greater visibility of such sites in the broader planning and heritage management processes described in Sections 4.3, 4.5 and 4.6.

4.6 Marine planning and development control

In recent years the UK's marine zone has become an increasingly exploited area. Oil and gas exploration and extraction, the establishment of renewable energy sources, the laying of undersea pipes and cables, aggregate extraction, and the ongoing use of existing port and harbour facilities by commercial shipping are all deemed to be important contributory industries to the economy and ongoing quality of life in the UK. The management, control and licensing of marine planning, development, and activity is provided for through the newly introduced MCAA in England, Wales, and Northern Ireland and the M(S)A in Scotland (see Section 4.3.1). In many cases the streamlined issuing of marine licenses will be undertaken by the relevant devolved authority (for further details see DEFRA 2008).

In addition to this, the JNAPC has formulated a Code of Practice for Seabed Development that is specifically designed to address and mitigate the threat posed to the archaeological resource contained in the marine zone (JNAPC 2008). This places the emphasis on suitable pre-disturbance assessment and consultation in order to identify any archaeological remains that may be at risk from the development. This can be followed up with formal archaeological investigation leading to preservation *in situ* (the favoured option), monitoring of any disturbance resulting from development, or the excavation and raising of archaeological material. The JNAPC's Code of Practice is supported by many of the key users/developers who operate in the UK's marine zone, including the British Marine Aggregate Producers Association, the British Ports Association, the British Wind Energy Association, the National Federation of Fishermen's

Organisations, the Renewable Power Association, the Salvage Association, and the United Kingdom Cable Protection Committee.

An important aspect of the MCAA and the associated MPS is the development of marine plans to provide for the management of English territorial waters. These will present the key policies and objectives of the MPS, over a minimum 20-year cycle, in terms that are locally relevant and include the views of local communities as well as other interested parties. Twelve areas covering English inshore and offshore waters have been proposed and are currently under consultation (DEFRA 2009, 22–3). In Scotland under the M(S)A, regional marine plans can be developed for Scottish Marine Regions.

4.6.1 Environmental assessment

4.6.1.i Environmental Impact Assessments

An Environmental Impact Assessment (EIA) must be undertaken before certain types of development may be granted consent. Under a European Directive (85/33/EEC as amended by 97/11/EC), a developer must compile and submit an Environmental Statement relating to the potential environmental impacts of any proposed development (also see Chapter 3). This statement should describe the likely significant effects of the development on the environment and any proposed mitigation measures that might be adopted. Statutory consultation and public comment should both occur before consent is given. Within the UK, the main heritage agencies (such as English Heritage or Historic Scotland, the latter being a 'consultation authority' on behalf of Scottish ministers) act as required statutory consultees for developments that may impact upon the marine historic environment. EIAs enable environmental factors (including heritage) to be given due consideration when taking into account planning applications. In this way, sustainability can be encouraged and the full consequences of any proposed development can be properly considered within the context of a single site. The concept of EIAs is now a central part of the control measures adopted by many of the primary developers in the marine zone (BMAPA & English Heritage 2003, 16; EMEC 2005; English Heritage 2006a).

4.6.1.ii Strategic Environmental Assessments

Strategic Environment Assessment (SEA) arises from the European Strategic Environmental Assessment Directive (Directive 2001/42/EC). Through this process environmental protection and sustainable development is integrated into large-scale or long-term development programmes. Areas such as agriculture, industry, energy, and transport all require SEA to be conducted as part of their planning/development procedures. More specific EIAs can then be placed within the context of these.

In relation to the UK's underwater cultural heritage, the main reasons for the employment of SEA stem from ongoing offshore oil and gas exploration and exploitation, as well as the increasing development of offshore wind farms

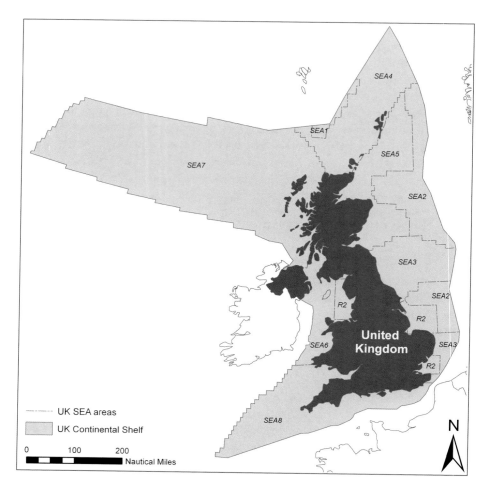

Figure 4.5 Strategic Environmental Assessment Areas in UK waters as originally conceived. Numbering indicates the order of consultation. R2 refers to the Round Two consultation relating to offshore wind farm developments (Image courtesy of HWTMA)

within UK territorial waters. The Department of Energy and Climate Change (formerly the Department of Trade and Industry) began a sequence of SEAs in 1999 that split the waters within the UK Continental Shelf into a number of sectors (Fig 4.5) which have subsequently been developed into a series of 'regional sea' areas.[13] It should be noted that while UK-sponsored seabed exploitation and development can extend to the limits of the Continental Shelf, none of the existing legislation relates to underwater cultural heritage located between the outer limit of territorial waters (at 12nm) and the Continental Shelf (Flemming 2002, 5). It could, however, be argued that the licensing and planning provision inherent in the EIA process would extend some form of protection beyond the territorial sea, providing developers follow EIA guidelines when formulating their activity in the offshore zone. Finally, shipwreck remains located in this zone that were raised and transported to UK territorial waters would fall under the Merchant Shipping Act and recovered material would be declared to the RoW.

Earlier SEAs have included assessment of specific elements of the marine archaeological resource, depending on the sector under assessment. For example,

SEA 2/3 includes a dedicated investigation into prehistoric archaeological remains (Flemming 2002), as distinct from the shipwreck archaeology occurring within the same area. The last SEA (SEA 8) was concerned with the assessing the impact of offshore energy development and includes a summary of the potential marine archaeological resource for the entire UK Continental Shelf.

4.6.2   The aggregates industry

The UK marine aggregates industry provides 20% of the sand and gravel used in construction projects in the UK as a whole and 50% of that used in London. In many cases, the use of marine aggregates is seen as preferable to aggregates extracted from terrestrial sources because of the reduced costs (economic and environmental) associated with transport by sea. Where aggregates are used in coastal defence works or beach replenishment they can be delivered directly to where they are required. Dredging activity is controlled by licenses that are administered by the MMO and The Crown Estate. The majority of licenses are for areas off the southern and eastern coasts of England, with other areas in the Bristol Channel and northern Irish Sea, and an inactive area in the Firth of Forth. Licensing conditions are monitored through use of a GPS-based electronic monitoring system which records the exact location of vessels undertaking aggregate extraction.

The potential impact of aggregate extraction on underwater cultural heritage is substantial and acknowledged (BMAPA & English Heritage 2003, 10). In the past there have been numerous cases of shipwrecks and other artefacts coming to light during the dredging process (eg Adams *et al* 1990). The importance of taking account of the impact of aggregate extraction is acknowledged by the BMAPA. The result of this has been the publication of a joint BMAPA/English Heritage document detailing the advised 'best practice' that should be adopted by aggregate extractors in order to take account of underwater cultural heritage (BMAPA & English Heritage 2003). This is accompanied by guidance on the reporting and recording of artefacts recovered during the extraction process (BMAPA & English Heritage 2005).

Prior to a license being granted marine geophysical data (side-scan sonar, bathymetric data, and so on) are reviewed during the EIA process (see Chapter 3) to gauge the historic environment interest of an area proposed for aggregate extraction, and appropriate mitigation measures (such as archaeological exclusion zones or archaeological reporting protocols), monitoring requirements, and licence conditions for the historic environment must be agreed with the appropriate heritage agency (eg English Heritage in England). Until recently the marine aggregates industry was able to make an active contribution through the ALSF to the mitigation and prevention of damage to the natural and historic marine environment via the levy of a tax of £1.60 per tonne on primary aggregate sales (see Section 4.6.2.i). Unfortunately, the UK government decided to discontinue the ALSF from the end of March 2011.

4.6.2.i The Aggregates Levy Sustainability Fund

The Aggregates Levy Sustainability Fund (ALSF) was introduced in April 2002 to provide funds to address environmental issues in areas affected by the extraction of aggregates. These funds included a ring-fenced allocation for marine initiatives within England distributed by English Heritage and the Centre for Environment, Fisheries and Aquaculture Science.[14] The latter distributed funding for non-heritage projects through the Marine Environment Protection Fund. In Wales, the ALSF was administered by the Planning Division of the Welsh Assembly government.

The main aim of the English Heritage ALSF programme within England was to reduce the impact of aggregate extraction on the historic environment through the commissioning of research and communication projects. Since its inception, the ALSF has provided funding for a wide range of projects concerned with the protection, management and investigation of maritime cultural heritage. These projects have included:

- wide-ranging investigation into the characterisation of sites likely to be affected by aggregate extraction;
- development of a joint protocol for reporting finds of archaeological interest by employees of the aggregates industry;
- implementing access and education workshops relating to maritime archaeology and marine aggregates;
- archaeological investigation and monitoring of a specific, threatened shipwreck lying within a licensed aggregate extraction area.

Since the initial two-year phase (Round One), which began in 2002, the ALSF has been extended to a second round lasting for three further years with an additional one-year extension. Round Three of the ALSF saw English Heritage receive £1.5m per annum until 2010/11, when the Fund ended in March 2011 (for further details see Chapter 2).

4.7 The UK marine science strategy

Although not a part of the heritage sector, the UK's marine scientific community obviously shares a great deal in common with it. This can be readily witnessed in areas such as marine management, but also in areas concerned with marine technology and the application of scientific processes to the marine environment. As a result of this, the recently published UK Marine Science Strategy is included here to provide a link to this important and complementary marine sector.[15]

The Marine Science Strategy sets out the general direction in which marine science should proceed across the whole of the UK between 2010 and 2025. It aims to provide a strategic framework for the delivery of world-class marine science across all parts of the UK marine science community. Unlike similar strategies (eg the NHPP), the Marine Science Strategy has been conceived for the whole of the UK, in conjunction with the UK government as well as the devolved administrations and key stakeholders in the scientific community. With this in mind, three high-level priority areas have been identified:

+ understanding how the marine ecosystem functions;
+ responding to climate change and its interaction with the marine environment;
+ sustaining and increasing ecosystem benefits.

As a result of the UK-wide implementation of the strategy, it will apply to all marine science that is funded by the departments, bodies, and devolved administrations that are represented on the co-ordination committee, encompassing all areas of the UK. The divergence in approaches between marine science and marine heritage is therefore notable. The former is adopting an approach whereby all parts of the UK subscribe to a single overarching vision, while the latter has, perhaps unconsciously, developed an approach based firmly on the empowerment of constituent parts of the UK, but which lacks overall consistency.

4.8 Summary

It is clear from this chapter that the situation in the UK relating to the protection and management of the marine historic environment is both complex and rapidly changing. Despite efforts to rationalise the situation, there is still a range of legislation that provides different levels of protection and ongoing management for different levels and classes of site. At a basic level, the UK's policy is to protect specific marine heritage assets once they have been identified as of sufficient significance. On the face of it, this may seem to be an unfavourable contrast with those countries that operate a policy of blanket protection of all underwater cultural heritage, whether known or unknown. However, the far-reaching planning, development, and environmental impact assessment processes that operate within UK territorial waters and the UK coastal zone mean that unknown heritage assets are unlikely to be destroyed prior to archaeological investigation and recording. The fact remains that a heritage asset may be wilfully destroyed if it is deemed less important or significant that the development taking place in its vicinity. Of ongoing interest is the evolution of heritage legislation at different speeds and with different outcomes within the devolved administrations of the UK. At the time of writing, it would be reasonable to say that the marine historic environment of Scotland is served by a better level of protection and management processes than that of England, Wales, and Northern Ireland. Consequently, the reader is advised to regularly consult the source material outlined here relating to legislative and policy reform in the devolved administrations of the individual countries.

Endnotes

1   www.culture.gov.uk.

2   www.mcga.gov.uk/c4mca/mcga-receiverofwreck.htm.

3   www.english-heritage.org.uk.

4   www.historic-scotland.gov.uk.

5   www.cadw.wales.gov.uk.

6   www.ni-environment.gov.uk.

7   www.jnapc.org.uk.

8   www.archaeologists.net and http://ifamag.wordpress.com/.

9   www.nauticalarchaeologysociety.org.

10   www.defra.gov.uk/publications/2011/09/30/pb13654-marine-policy-statement/.

11   www.english-heritage.org.uk/professional/advice/conservation-principles/. ConservationPrinciples/; www.cadw.wales.gov.uk/historicenvironment/conservation/conservationprinciples/?lang=en.

12   For more details see www.english-heritage.org.uk/professional/designation/national-heritage-protection-plan/.

13   www.offshore-sea.org.uk.

14   www.english-heritage.org.uk/professional/research/coastal-and-maritime/aslf-marine/.

15   www.defra.gov.uk/environment/marine/science/mscc.htm.

CHAPTER 5

Maritime cultural heritage conventions and the UK

This chapter summarises the principal international conventions relating to underwater cultural heritage that have been acknowledged or ratified by the UK. These international conventions impact on the management and protection of the cultural resource. The account presented here is by no means exhaustive and should serve only to familiarise the reader with the main conventions that they are likely to encounter.

Particular emphasis is placed on the Council of Europe's European Landscape Convention (ELC). The ELC is the first international instrument devoted exclusively to the protection, management, and planning of landscape in its entirety, and is an initiative that bridges all components of the historic environment. It is certainly relevant to maritime-related issues: as well as 'land' and 'inland water', the scope of the ELC specifically includes 'marine areas' and defines them as 'coastal waters and the territorial sea' (Article 2.43). It takes a holistic landscape/seascape approach. Within this context, particular emphasis in this book is placed on the connections between ELC and the Historic Seascape Characterisation programme run by English Heritage as a case study.

As with the UK-specific legislation described in the previous chapter, the recent nature of developments described in this section mean that coherent quantification of the likely long-term effects of implementation or non-implementation is often difficult to predict. Readers are therefore encouraged to use the links to sources of further information in order to establish the exact situation at the time of reading.

5.1 Conventions relating to the marine cultural heritage

5.1.1 The United Nations Convention on the Law of the Sea (1982)

The legal framework relating to the marine environment is set out by the United Nations Convention on the Law of the Sea (UNCLOS), which the UK ratified in 1997.[1] The UNCLOS sets out five different zones within which different legal regimes apply (Fig 5.1). All of these zones are measured from a 'baseline', which is taken as the low water mark as marked on large-scale charts recognised by each State.

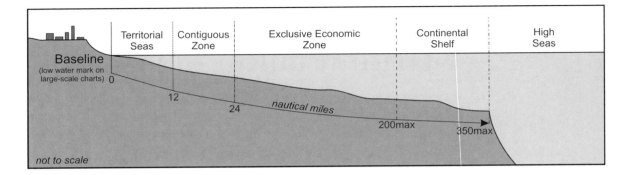

Within the image:

Baseline
(low water mark on large-scale charts)

| Territorial Seas | Contiguous Zone | Exclusive Economic Zone | Continental Shelf | High Seas |

0
12
24 *nautical miles*
200max
350max

not to scale

5.1.1.i Territorial seas

The territorial sea extends to a maximum limit of 12nm, measured from the baseline (Fig 5.1). Within this zone the State has exclusive regulatory rights to all marine activity, including those related to maritime archaeology. The UK's territorial sea area is illustrated in Fig 1.1. Further information regarding statutory curatorial responsibility for the marine historic environment within this area is given in Chapter 4.

5.1.1.ii Contiguous zone

Lying adjacent to the territorial sea, the contiguous zone extends to a maximum distance of 24nm from the baseline (Fig 5.1). Within this zone a State may control, prevent, and punish any infringement of its customs, fiscal, immigration, or sanitary laws as though they occurred within its territory or territorial waters (ie 12nm). A State may consider the recovery of archaeological or historical objects found in this area to have taken place within its territorial sea (ie 12nm). Consequently a State may choose to extend its ability to regulate activity to 24nm. In the UK, present legislation (see later in this section) includes underwater cultural heritage located only within the territorial sea (ie 12nm).

5.1.1.iii Exclusive economic zone

Lying adjacent to and beyond the contiguous zone, the exclusive economic zone extends to a maximum distance of 200nm from the baseline (Fig 5.1). Its main function is to allow the State to exploit the natural resources within this area. Other States continue to have freedoms within this zone, including marine scientific research. However, maritime archaeology is not currently considered as falling under this bracket of marine scientific research and so the extent to which it can be regulated by the State is unclear (cf Bowens 2008, 46). The UK does not currently seek to regulate such activity within its exclusive economic zone.

Figure 5.1 Illustration of legal difference in sea areas according to UNCLOS (Image courtesy of HWTMA)

Within a marine context, landscape perspective initiatives are being developed following the Marine and Coastal Access Act 2009 (see Chapter 4). For example, the Act contains provisions for the creation of a new type of MPA in England called a Marine Conservation Zone (MCZ). MCZs are designed to protect nationally important marine wildlife, habitats, geology, and geomorphology. Despite strong lobbying of government for MCZs to be able to be designated for cultural heritage, this was not included within the legislation, and so associated historical or cultural features may derive protection from MCZs only indirectly: under Clause 117, the Secretary of State may consider historic or archaeological remains under the 'social consequences' of an MCZ designation. Thus the only way cultural heritage can be 'protected' by this initiative is if it happens to be associated with designated biological communities.

MCZs can be designated anywhere in English inshore and UK offshore waters. In English inshore and English, Welsh and Northern Irish offshore waters, MCZs have been identified through the Marine Conservation Zone Project. The Marine Conservation Zone Project was set up in 2009 and consisted of four Regional Projects covering the South-West, Irish Sea, North Sea and Eastern Channel.[9] In Welsh inshore waters it is predicted that there will be a small number of MCZs affording a high level of protection. Site selection is being managed by the Welsh Government engaging widely with the public and sea user interests. Sites will be selected to protect not just the rare and threatened but also a representative range of marine wildlife together with its overlying water and associated flora, fauna, and historical or cultural features, which are protected by legal means.

5.2.2 English Heritage and Historic Seascape Characterisation (HSC) Programme in context with the European Landscape Convention

Characterisation is a tool for managing change affecting the historic dimension of the landscape (Fairclough 2006a, b). It was first applied in England, bringing together ideas already circulating in landscape archaeology and landscape management with an increased need for informed, forward-looking spatial planning at a landscape scale (see Clark et al 2004). The Historic Landscape Characterisation (HLC) programme is a powerful tool that provides a framework for broadening the understanding of the whole landscape and contributes to decisions shaping tomorrow's landscapes (Clark et al 2004; English Heritage 2004). Now well established in 'land-based' contexts, HLC projects provide generalised overviews of the origins and development of the present landscape. This enables the management of the inevitable ongoing changes affecting it and informs about the cultural context in which those changes need to be accommodated.

As on land, large-scale change and development pressures are increasing on the coasts and in the seas of the UK, including society's growing demand for marine aggregates and offshore renewable energy. The ability to assess and respond to impacts on the coastal and marine historic environment relies extensively on

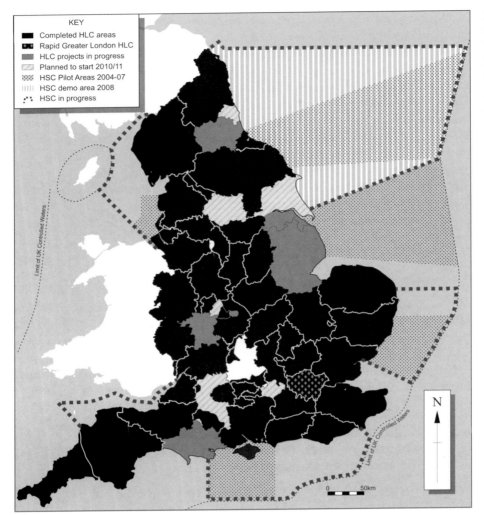

KEY
■ Completed HLC areas
▨ Rapid Greater London HLC
▨ HLC projects in progress
▨ Planned to start 2010/11
▨ HSC Pilot Areas 2004-07
⦚ HSC demo area 2008
⋰ HSC in progress

Fig 5.2 Map of the areas characterised by the Historic Seascape Characterisation Programme in England, at the time of writing (Image courtesy of English Heritage)

mapped locations of known specific features and recorded find spots. While these specific 'point' data will always remain invaluable in minimising impacts on the rare or otherwise special, they are less effective at conveying the typical historic processes that have influenced the development of areas and the roles of human activity in shaping the environment. An area-based understanding of character is essential if the historic dimension of the landscape is to play its full role in the management of change. English Heritage has developed Historic Seascape Characterisation (HSC) to extend the principles underpinning HLC to the intertidal and marine zones (Fig 5.2). Consolidation of a robust HSC method was completed in 2007, following closely upon the transfer of statutory curatorial responsibility for historic environment matters within England's Territorial Waters to English Heritage (see Roberts & Trow 2002). Currently, English Heritage is implementing the HSC method in project-based stages around England's territorial sea and adjacent waters to the limit of the UK's Controlled

Waters (see Fig 5.2). Characterisation of the historic seascape within these zones will be a powerful tool in enabling English Heritage to meet its responsibilities relating to management, research, and improved public understanding of the historic sites and landscapes of England, both land and sea, in addition to its advisory role to the UK government on such matters. HSC is particularly timely following the enactment of the Marine and Coastal Access Act (2009), which introduces a system of marine spatial planning that reinforces the need to develop area-based understandings of both the historic and the natural environments.

Although not discussed as part of this book it is worth noting that, in the UK, there are other initiatives also involving landscape/seascape characterisation, such as the Dorset Land and Seascape Assessment[10] and the assessment of the character of Wales' coastal landscapes and their sensitivity to offshore developments.[11]

HSC, in common with HLC, follows the fundamental principles (published in Clark *et al* 2004) that underpin historic characterisation:

+ HLC characterises the present landscape in terms of its context or origin;
+ HLC-based research and understanding are concerned with areas;
+ all aspects of the landscape are part of the landscape character;
+ characterisation is a matter of interpretation, not record, and perception rather than facts;
+ characterisation aims to manage change;
+ HLC process is transparent, with clearly articulated records of data and methods used;
+ HLC maps and text are jargon-free and easily accessible to users;
+ HLC results should be capable of integration into other environmental and heritage management datasets.

The ELC embodies those same concepts (see earlier in the section) that are already at the heart of historic landscape and seascape characterisation, including the central roles of human activity in creating landscapes and of human perception in defining them. This is clearly expressed in the ELC definition of landscape quoted above: 'an area, as perceived by people, whose character is the result of the action and interaction of natural and/or human factors'. English Heritage defines the term 'seascape' following the ELC definition for 'landscape', understanding seascapes as the subset of landscape perceptions that have a distinctly maritime perspective and relate to the coastal and marine zones. Hence, the ELC encourages the understanding and management of dynamic landscapes, recognising their diversity and the complex interplays of cultural and natural forces that influence their perception. The ELC provides strong motivation for characterising coastal and marine landscapes and HSC offers an effective tool in meeting ELC obligations by building a comprehensive approach to historic seascapes and recognising that change is inevitable, often desirable, and needs to be accommodated.

The ELC requires its ratifying parties to recognise 'landscapes in law as an essential component of people's surroundings, an expression of the diversity of their shared cultural and natural heritage, and a foundation of their identity' (Article 5). This central role of human activities and perceptions in creating and defining landscapes reinforces concepts already at the heart of HLC and HSC (Clark *et al* 2004; English Heritage 2004; Hooley 2007). English Heritage also published an Action Plan for implementing the requirements of the ELC across its own activities (English Heritage 2009). This plan seeks opportunities to promote better recognition of the historic dimension of landscape in the marine zone through the promotion of HSC and the development of new legislation and procedures.

The scope of the ELC specifically includes 'marine areas' as well as 'land' and 'inland water' (ELC, Article 2) and, in common with HLC and HSC, it takes a holistic approach, concerning all areas and including 'landscapes that might be considered outstanding as well as everyday or degraded landscapes' (ELC, Article 2).

The ELC requires each party where it is in force 'to identify its own landscapes throughout its territory' and 'to analyse their characteristics' (ELC, Article 6). These are fundamental tasks central to HLC and HSC (see earlier in this section). The applications which HLC and HSC are designed to inform (see Clark *et al* 2004) are also directly aligned with the requirements in the ELC to analyse 'the forces and pressures transforming those characteristics' (ELC, Article 6) and 'to establish and implement landscape policies aimed at landscape protection, management and planning' (ELC, Article 5).

5.3 Summary

This chapter has discussed the main international conventions that relate to underwater cultural heritage and have been acknowledged or ratified by the UK. Within this corpus of material, the reader's attention is drawn to the likely future importance of the 2001 UNESCO convention as a means of establishing internationally adopted standards and practices for the protection of underwater cultural heritage. The chapter has also placed particular emphasis on the ELC since it bridges all components of the historic environment. The Historic Seascape Characterisation programme, which offers a tool in meeting ELC obligations, was used as an example of how this Europe-wide convention can be extended and applied to the marine zone of a specific region.

Endnotes

1   The full text of the convention is available at www.un.org/Depts/los/convention_agreements/convention_overview_convention.htm.

2   The full text of the convention is available at www.conventions.coe.int/Treaty/en/Treaties/html/143.htm.

3   For further information see www.unesco.org/en/underwater-cultural-heritage/.

4   www.coe.int/t/dg4/cultureheritage/heritage/landscape/default_en.asp.

5   See www.helm.org.uk/server/show/nav.20574 and www.naturalengland.org.uk/ourwork/landscape/protection/europeanconvention/default.aspx respectively.

6   For further details see www.uklandscapeconference.org/.

7   (see www.coe.int/t/dg4/cultureheritage/heritage/landscape/default_en.asp)

8   See www.naturalengland.org.uk/ourwork/campaigns/default.aspx.

9   For the south-west see www.finding-sanctuary.org/page/project-area, for the Irish Sea www.irishseaconservation.org.uk/, for the North Sea www.netgainmcz.org/ and for the south-east see www.balancedseas.org/page/home.html.

10 For further details see www.maps.dorsetforyou.com/landscape/ and www.dorsetforyou.com/C-SCOPE.

11 For further details see www.ccw.gov.uk/landscape--wildlife/protecting-our-landscape/seascapes/seascape-assessment-of-wales.aspx.

CHAPTER 6

Conclusions

Smaller scale events are not purely contingent on local circumstances, but provide a scale of analysis focusing on the points at which the strategies and histories of individuals meet broader economic and cultural forces. Broader processes would not exist without local forces and events, so that the study of the local can provide us with new insights into broader forces.

(Gosden & Knowles 2001)

... whatever the differences between land and maritime archaeologies with respect to environment and method, they do not and should not constitute barriers within theory, analysis and interpretation.

(Adams 2006)

6.1 Introduction

This book has provided the reader with a brief overview of how marine archaeology fits within archaeology as a discipline, its development through time, the extent of the UK marine zone, the main sectors involved in marine archaeology, the key areas of work on which they are concentrating and issues and challenges that these sectors are currently facing. It has also discussed the basic steps that professional archaeologists follow on marine projects, the administration, formal policy and legal context relating to the protection and management of underwater cultural heritage within the UK, and the principal international conventions that relate to underwater cultural heritage and have been acknowledged or ratified by the UK.

6.2 The resource

The previous chapters have illustrated the complex and varied character of the marine historic environment. Its wealth and diversity in the UK is immense and its potential to inform on many aspects of human development and interaction needs to be further explored. However, the details presented here are by no means exhaustive and should serve only to familiarise the reader with the main issues related to marine archaeology.

Despite recent advances, there is still limited knowledge of the marine cultural resource, mainly related to its location, nature, and extent. The nature and scale of palaeogeographic and palaeoenvironmental change in the UK continental margins is of particular importance to the process of reconstruction, as it can radically alter our perception of prehistoric and historic timescales. Therefore, there is a need to understand the nature of the UK continental margins and the short- and long-term processes that affect them.

Submerged landscapes are now a major focus of underwater archaeological investigation as they potentially contain a large proportion of the prehistoric record of human settlement (Flemming 2004; Quinn *et al* 2000). The UK continental shelf is under intense developmental pressure from a range of 'threats', including mineral extraction and the direct impact of construction projects (Dix *et al* 2004). On account of these threats it is imperative that further research is undertaken to enable a deeper understanding of submerged prehistoric landscapes before they are lost forever as a result not only of human action but also of natural erosive processes. The study of submerged prehistoric landscapes is essential to the study of past human evolution, migration, and global dispersal. Further study of these landscapes will help to define the extent and character of the resource and address issues of long-term management and hence encourage the sustainable use of the seas and conservation of marine ecosystems.

The integration of different scales of analysis is needed if archaeologists want to achieve a more comprehensive understanding of the past. In this sense, marine archaeological sites need to be understood within their broader context by addressing the complex web of socio-political factors which shaped them.

The marine archaeology sector is also facing an archive crisis. The completion of any archaeological project, whether research or development-led, should include the deposition of the full archive within a public museum or repository. While theoretically archives from the marine zone are subject to the same standards as those generated from terrestrial investigations (see Brown 2007), the fate of marine archaeological archives is not always clear, as there are few museums willing or able to hold and curate such archives (for further information see 'Securing a Future for Maritime Archaeological Archives' project.[']) The lack of a coordinated collection of marine archaeological archives and of established reference collections has negatively affected the development of the discipline and related research interests, hampering our understanding of the significance of this resource to the history of the UK.

6.3 The marine historic environment: finite and non-renewable

This book has highlighted the unique, finite, and non-renewable nature of the archaeological resource, which makes its preservation for present and future generations crucial. Salvage activities have a detrimental impact not only on the cultural resource but also on the development of the archaeological discipline and the profession as a whole. Salvage activities are not within recognised best archaeological practice (IfA 2010; UNESCO 2001). Archaeological remains should in the first instance be left *in situ* unless they are under threat. This principle is clearly articulated in Rule 1 of the UNESCO Convention on the Protection of the Underwater Cultural Heritage Annex. Although the UK has not ratified the Convention, it supports the implementation of the provisions of the Annex (see British government statement circulated by the Foreign and Commonwealth Office on 31 October 2001; Chapter 5, endnote 3). Therefore, within this context, proactive approaches are needed which should encompass (for further details see Adams 2007):

- management: prioritising quantification (including extent and character) of the resource;
- communication and education: establishing outreach and educational programmes to allow public access to research outcomes as well as raising public awareness and understanding of heritage in the UK. These programmes could also contribute to changing perceptions, with the help of the media, not only of the general public but of legislators and administrators;
- research: proactive, rather than reactive, research is needed. This should involve the development of both theory and method in response to new source material.

Since archaeology is interdisciplinary in nature it has, throughout its history, absorbed theories and methods from other subjects which have shaped the discipline today. While theories and methods develop through time, the core aims of the discipline remain relatively unchanged (for further discussion see Adams 2007). Concomitant with these aims are the ethical, academic, and professional criteria which govern the practice of the discipline (Adams 2007, 54), as defined in the Annex of the UNESCO Convention on the Protection of the Underwater Cultural Heritage.

6.4 Final thoughts

Archaeology is the study of the past through the material remains that people have left behind. As archaeologists our goal is to 'rediscover' the past and interpret it in the light of a present that it continues to shape. Archaeologists analyse human interactions with the environment regardless of the context in which the research takes place: prehistoric, historic, terrestrial, or marine. If archaeologists wish to gain a better and more comprehensive understanding of past human activities, however, an appreciation is needed of the complexity of society, of its features, and of changes in the material remains that people leave behind. This can be achieved through pluralistic, interdisciplinary, and broad perspectives. Archaeological studies, therefore, need to transcend the conventional boundaries between marine and terrestrial, history and prehistory.

As discussed in Chapter 2, archaeology comprises three central concepts: objects, landscapes/seascapes, and the interpretations of these reached by archaeologists now and in the future (Gamble 2001, 15). This activity comes with responsibilities and challenges. Despite the current challenges that the marine archaeology sector is facing, archaeology continues to help form new ideas about the past (Johnson 2000, 9). Whether it is carried out by professional or voluntary practitioners, marine archaeological work currently involves challenges and debates, and will continue to do so. It is through these challenges and debates that the archaeological discipline grows as a whole.

Endnotes

1   www.hwtma.org.uk/maritime-archaeological-archives.

CHAPTER 7

Glossary and Guidance and resources

7.1 Glossary

Terms are listed alphabetically. Where applicable, the related legislation is included in brackets (see Chapter 4 for further details).

Ancient Monument (*Ancient Monuments and Archaeological Areas Act*)
Defined as any structure, work, site (including and site comprising, or comprising the remains of, any vehicle, vessel, aircraft or other movable structure or part thereof), garden or area which is of historic, architectural, traditional, artistic or archaeological interest.

Coastal zone
Area of landscape immediately adjacent to the sea. The coastal zone extends seaward as far as the mean low water mark. Its landward extent is harder to define, but has varied between 100m and 1.5km when defined during coastal zone assessment surveys.

Controlled Site (*Protection of Military Remains Act*)
Restricted area resulting from designation under the PMRA. The MOD can specify the co-ordinates of an area that encompass the location of a military vessel lost during the last 200 years. No diving or salvage activity may take place within this area without permission from the MOD.

Derelict (*Merchant Shipping Act*)
Property (vessel or cargo) that has been abandoned and deserted at sea by those in charge of it, without any hope of recovery.

Designation (*Protection of Wrecks Act*)
Designation applies to all types of designated assets. For example, designation of a historic asset can occur if the site of a vessel lying wrecked on or in the seabed is of such historical, archaeological or artistic significance that it ought to be protected from unauthorised interference. The site may also be designated on account of any objects contained or formerly contained in the vessel that may be lying on the seabed in or near to the designated asset.

Flotsam (*Merchant Shipping Act*)

Goods lost from a ship that has sunk which are recoverable because they have remained afloat.

Historic Marine Protection Area (*Marine Scotland Bill*)

An area may be designated as a Historic MPA for the purpose of preserving a marine historic asset of national importance located, or which Scottish ministers are satisfied may be located, in the area.

Intertidal zone

The area that lies between the high water mark and the low water mark of ordinary spring tides.

Jetsam (*Merchant Shipping Act*)

Goods cast overboard in order to lighten a vessel in danger of sinking, notwithstanding that afterwards the vessel may sink.

Lagan (*Merchant Shipping Act*)

Goods cast overboard from a ship (that subsequently sinks) that are buoyed in order to allow later recovery.

Licenses (*Protection of Wrecks Act*)

Under the terms of the PWA licenses may be granted to access and work on designated wrecks. Licenses may be granted only to individuals who are competent and properly equipped to carry out salvage operations in a manner appropriate to the historical, archaeological or artistic importance of the wreck.

Marine Historic Asset (*Marine Scotland Bill*)

A marine historic asset is defined by the M(S)A (section 73(5)) as any of the following:

- A vessel, vehicle or aircraft (or part of any of a vessel, vehicle or aircraft);
- The remains of a vessel, vehicle or aircraft (or part of such remains);
- An object contained in, or formerly contained in, a vessel, vehicle or aircraft;
- A building or other structure (or part of a building or structure);
- A cave or excavation;
- A deposit or artefact (whether or not formerly part of the cargo of a ship) or any other thing which evidences, or groups of things which evidence, previous human activity.

The UK Marine Policy Statement also includes reference to 'heritage assets'; these are broadly defined as: 'those elements of the historic environment – buildings, monuments, sites or landscapes – that have been positively identified as holding a degree of significance meriting consideration are called "heritage assets".' (http://www.defra.gov.uk/publications/files/pb3654-marine-policy-statement-110316.pdf, 24)

Marine zone
Area of the sea extending seaward from the mean low water mark. The marine zone is often split into an inshore zone, from the low water mark to the twelve-mile limit of territorial waters, and an offshore zone, which covers the remaining distance to the continental shelf (where permissible).

Protected Place (*Protection of Military Remains Act*)
Under the PMRA, the MOD may designate by name the remains of a military vessel (British or otherwise) that sank after the outbreak of World War One. The exact location of the vessel does not have to be specified. A Protected Place may be visited and dived upon, but it is an offence to disturb the remains.

7.2 Guidance and resources

ADS ALSF online http://ads.ahds.ac.uk/project/alsf/
The Archaeology Data Service (ADS) is currently archiving all English Heritage Aggregates Levy Sustainability Fund (ALSF) projects. The aim of the project is to disseminate on the web and secure for the long term a key set of research and management documents produced for English Heritage by a wide range of ALSF-funded projects.

Historic Environment Local Management www.helm.org.uk/index.php
Historic Environment Local Management (HELM) was established by English Heritage in 2004 to provide easily accessible information, training and guidance to decision-makers within local authorities, regional agencies and national organisations. The HELM website contains the most recent English Heritage publications as well as the most recent information on Heritage Protection Reform. In addition, there are examples of good practice case studies and publications from across England.

Office of Public Sector Information www.opsi.gov.uk/legislation
The Office of Public Sector Information provides (OPSI) electronic access to the various legislative Acts described above. These are available for both UK-wide Acts of Parliament and for legislation passed through the devolved administrations. The site is fully searchable and provides either the original Act or an updated version that takes into account amendments or revision made since the original was enacted.

Scottish Coastal Archaeology and the Problem of Erosion Trust www.scapetrust.org
The Scottish Coastal Archaeology and the Problem of Erosion (SCAPE) Trust was established in 2001. It is a charitable company that aims to research, conserve and promote the archaeology of the Scottish coast. It has been responsible for conducting the CZASs sponsored by Historic Scotland. These surveys are available to download from the SCAPE website.

Bibliography

ACHWS, 2009 *Annual Report 2008 (April 2008–March 2009)*. DCMS: English Heritage for Advisory Committee on Historic Wreck Sites

Adams, J, 2001 Ships and boats as archaeological source material, *World Archaeol*, **32**(3), 292–310

Adams, J, 2002 Maritime archaeology, in C Orser Jr (ed) *Encyclopaedia of Historical Archaeology*. London: Routledge, 328–30

Adams, J, 2003 *Ships, innovation and social change: aspects of carvel shipbuilding in northern Europe 1450–1850*. Stockholm: Stockholm University

Adams, J, 2006 From the water margins to the centre ground? *J Maritime Archaeol*, **1**, 1–8

Adams, J, 2007 Alchemy or science? Compromising archaeology in the deep sea, *J Maritime Archaeol*, **2**, 48–56

Adams, J, Van Holk, A F L & Maarleveld, T, 1990 *Dredgers and archaeology: shipfinds from the slufter*. Alphen aan den Rijn: Ministerie van Welzijn, Volksgezondheid en Cultuur

Auer, J & Firth, A, 2007 The 'Gresham Ship': an interim report on a 16th century wreck from Princess Channel, Thames Estuary, *Post-Medieval Archaeol*, **41**(2), 222–41

Babits, L & Van Tilburg, H (eds), 1998 *Maritime archaeology: a reader of substantive and theoretical contributions*. New York: Plenum Press

Bailey, G, 2004 The wider significance of submerged archaeological sites and their relevance to world prehistory, in N Flemming (ed) *Submarine prehistoric archaeology of the North Sea: research priorities and collaboration with industry*, CBA Res Rep **141**. York: English Heritage and Council for British Archaeology, 3–10

Barstad, J, 2002 Underwater archaeology in the 20th century: filling in the gaps, in J Barstad & C Ruppé (eds) *International handbook of underwater archaeology*. London/New York: Plenum Press, 3–16

Bass, G, 1966 *Archaeology underwater*. London: Thames and Hudson

Bates, M, Bates, C R & Briant, R, 2007 Bridging the gap: a terrestrial view of shallow marine sequences and the importance of the transition zone, *J Archaeol Sci*, **34**, 1537–51

Bates, R, Lawrence, M, Dean, M & Robertson, P, 2011 Geophysical methods for wreck-site monitoring: the Rapid Archaeological Site Surveying and Evaluation (RASSE) Programme, *Int J Naut Archaeol*, Online Early View. doi: 10.1111/j.1095-9270.2010.00298.x Accessed 7 July 2011

Bayley, J, Crossley, D & Ponting, M (eds), 2008 *Metals and metalworking: a research framework for archaeometallurgy*, Historical Metallurgy Society Occasional Publication **6**. London: Historical Metallurgy Society

Bell, M & Warren, G, forthcoming Mesolithic, in J Ransley, L Blue, J Dix & F Sturt (eds) *Future studies in maritime archaeology: England's maritime and marine historic environment resource assessment and research agenda*. Southampton: English Heritage

Bell, M, Manning, S & Nayling, N, 2009 Dating the Mesolithic of western Britain: a test of some evolutionary assumptions, in P Crombé, M van Strydonck, J Sergant, M Boudin & M Bats (eds) *Chronology and evolution within the Mesolithic of north-west Europe*. Newcastle upon Tyne: Cambridge Scholars Publishing, 615–34

Bevan, J, 1996 *The Infernal Diver*. Portsmouth: Submex Ltd

Blundell, O, 1909 Notice of the examination, by means of a diving-dress, of the artificial island, or crannog, of Eilean Muireach, in the south end of Loch Ness, *Proc Soc Antiq Scotl*, **43**, 159–64

Blundell, O, 1910 On further examination of artificial islands in the Beauly Firth, Loch Bruiach, Loch Moy, Loch Garry, Loch Lundy, Loch Oich, Loch Lochy and Loch Treig, *Proc Soc Antiq Scotl*, **44**, 12–33

BMAPA & English Heritage, 2003 *Marine aggregate dredging and the historic environment: guidance note*. London: BMAPA & English Heritage

BMAPA & English Heritage, 2005 *Protocol for reporting finds of archaeological interest*, prepared by Wessex Archaeology on behalf of BMAPA & English Heritage, Available: http://ads.ahds. ac.uk/catalogue/projArch/alsf/search_maritime.cfm or http://www.wessexarch.co.uk/projects/ marine/bmapa/arch-interest.html Accessed 6 July 2011

Bowens, A (ed), 2008 *Archaeology underwater: the NAS guide to principles and practice*, 2nd rev edn. Oxford: Wiley Blackwell

Bradford, E, 1982 *The story of the Mary Rose*. London: Hamish Hamilton

Breen, C, Barton, K, Callaghan, C, Forsythe, W, Quinn, R et al, 2001 *Integrated marine investigation on the historic shipwreck La Surveillante*. Coleraine, Northern Ireland: University of Ulster

Broadwater, J, 2002 Timelines of underwater archaeology, in J Barstad & C Ruppé (eds) *International handbook of underwater archaeology*. London/New York: Plenum Press, 17–24

Brown, D, 2007 *Archaeological archives: a guide to best practice in creation, compilation, transfer and curation*. Reading: Institute of Field Archaeologists

Camidge, K, 2009 HMS *Colossus*, an experimental site stabilization, *Conservation and Management of Archaeological Sites*, **11**(2), 161–88

Chambers, W & Chambers, R, 1881 *Encyclopaedia – A Dictionary of Universal Knowledge for the People*. Philadelphia: J B Lippincott & Co

Clark, J, Darlington, J & Fairclough, G, 2004 *Using Historic Landscape Characterisation: English Heritage's review of HLC applications 2002–03*. London & Preston: English Heritage & Lancashire County Council

Connah, G, 1993 *The archaeology of Australia's history*. Cambridge: Cambridge University Press

Council of Europe (ed), 2008 *Heritage and beyond*. Strasbourg: Council of Europe

DCLG, 2000 *Environmental Impact Assessment: a guide to procedures*. London: DCLG Available: http://www.communities.gov.uk/publications/planningandbuilding/ environmentalimpactassessment Accessed 7 July 2011

DCLG, 2006 *Environmental Impact Assessment: a guide to good practice and procedures. A consultation paper*. London: DCLG Available: http://www.communities.gov.uk/archived/ publications/planningandbuilding/environmentalimpactassessment Accessed 7 July 2011

DCLG, 2010 *Planning Policy Statement 5: Planning for the Historic Environment: historic environment planning practice guide*. London: DCLG Available: http://www.communities.gov.uk/ publications/planningandbuilding/pps5 Accessed 7 July 2011

DCLG, 2011 *National Planning Policy Framework*. London: DCLG Available: http://www. communities.gov.uk/documents/planningandbuilding/pdf/2116950.pdf Accessed 14 August 2012

DCMS, 2007 *Heritage Protection for the 21st Century*. London: HMSO

DCMS, 2010 Department for Culture, Media and Sport Business Plan 2011–2015. London: DCMS (Version Nov 2010) Available: http://www.culture.gov.uk/publications/7545.aspx Accessed 7 July 2011

DEFRA, 2006 *Shoreline Management Plan Guidance: aims and requirements*. London: Department for Environment, Food and Rural Affairs Available: http://www.defra.gov.uk/ publications/2011/06/10/pb11726-shoreline-guidance/ Accessed 7 July 2011

DEFRA, 2008 *Managing our marine resources – licensing under the Marine Bill*. London: DEFRA Available: www.bwea.com/pdf/offshore/Marine%20licensing%20publication.pdf Accessed 7 July 2011

DEFRA, 2009 *European Landscape Convention – a framework for implementation in England*. London: DEFRA Available: http://www.naturalengland.org.uk/ourwork/landscape/ protection/europeanconvention/default.aspx Accessed 7 July 2011

Delbourgo, J, 2007 Underwater-works: voyages and visions of the submarine, *Endeavour*, **31**(3), 115–20

Dellino-Musgrave, V, 2006 *Maritime archaeology and social relations: British action in the southern hemisphere*. New York: Springer Press

Dellino-Musgrave, V, 2007 Marine aggregate dredging and the historic environment: joint initiatives for a sustainable management, in V Mastone (ed) *ACUA underwater archaeology proceedings 2007*. Advisory Council on Underwater Archaeology, 33–46

Dellino-Musgrave, V & Ransley, J, forthcoming Maritime and Marine Historic Environment Research Framework: resource assessment – post-medieval & early modern (c. 1600–1850 AD), in J Ransley, L Blue, J Dix & F Sturt (eds) *Future studies in maritime archaeology: England's maritime and marine historic environment resource assessment and research agenda*. Southampton: English Heritage

Dellino-Musgrave, V, Gupta, S & Russell, M, 2009 Marine aggregates and archaeology: a golden harvest? *Conservation and Management of Archaeological Sites*, **11**(1), 29–42

Dix, J, Quinn, R & Westley, K, 2004 A reassessment of the archaeological potential of continental shelves. Southampton: Southampton University, Available: http://www.soton.ac.uk/ archaeology/research/projects/reassessment_arch_cont_shelves.html Accessed June 2011

DOENI, 2010 *A Northern Ireland Marine Bill – Policy Proposals. Consultation Document*. Belfast: DOENI Available: http://www.doeni.gov.uk/index/protect_the_environment/water/marine_ bill_.htm Accessed 7 July 2011

Dolwick, J, 2008 In search of the social: steamboats, square wheels, reindeer and other things, *J Maritime Archaeol* **3**(1), 15–41

Dromgoole, S, 2006 United Kingdom, in S Dromgoole (ed) *The protection of the underwater cultural heritage: national perspectives in light of the UNESCO Convention 2001*. Leiden/Boston: Martinus Nijhoff Publishers, 313–50

Dromgoole, S, 2010 Revisiting the relationship between marine scientific research and the underwater cultural heritage, *The International Journal of Marine and Coastal Law*, **25**, 33–61

Dunkley, M, 2008 *Protected wreck sites at risk: a risk management handbook*. London: English Heritage

Edwards, R J & Brooks, A J, 2008 The Island of Ireland: Drowning the Myth of an Irish Land-bridge? in J J Davenport, D P Sleeman & P C Woodman (eds), *Mind the Gap: Postglacial Colonisation of Ireland, Special Supplement to The Irish Naturalists' Journal*, 19–34

Embree, S & Stevens, J, 2005 *English Heritage research agenda: an introduction to English Heritage's research themes and programmes*. London: English Heritage

EMEC, 2005 *Environmental impact assessment (EIA) guidance for developers at the European Marine Energy Centre*. Stromness, Orkney: European Marine Energy Centre

English Heritage, 2001 *Enabling development and the conservation of heritage assets*. London: English Heritage

English Heritage, 2004 *Conservation bulletin: characterisation*. London: English Heritage

English Heritage, 2005 *Making the past part of our future: English Heritage strategy 2005–2010*. London: English Heritage

English Heritage, 2006a *Ports: the impact of development on the maritime historic environment*. London: English Heritage

English Heritage, 2006b *Management of Research Projects in the Historic Environment. The MoRPHE Project Managers' Guide*. English Heritage: Swindon. Available http://www. english-heritage.org.uk/publications/morphe-project-managers-guide/ Accessed 7 July 2011

English Heritage, 2008 *Conservation principles: policies and guidance for the sustainable management of the historic environment*. London: English Heritage

English Heritage, 2009 *The European Landscape Convention: the English Heritage action plan for implementation*. London: English Heritage

English Heritage, 2011 *National Heritage Protection Plan. Priorities for Action (version May 2011)*. London: English Heritage

Erlandson, J, 2001 The archaeology of aquatic adaptations: paradigms for a new millennium, *J Archaeol Res*, **9**, 287–350

Evans, C & Hodder, I, 2006 *Woodland archaeology: Neolithic sites at Haddenham*. London: English Heritage

Fairclough, G, 2006a From assessment to characterisation, in J Hunter & I Ralston (eds) *Archaeological resource management in the UK: an introduction*, 2nd edn. Stroud: Sutton, 250–70

Fairclough, G, 2006b A new landscape for cultural heritage management: characterisation as a management tool, in L Lozny (ed) *Landscapes under pressure: theory and practice of cultural heritage research and preservation*. New York: Springer Press, 55–74

Fitch, S, Gaffney, V & Ramsay, E, 2010 West Coast Palaeolandscape Pilot Project. Unpublished manuscript, University of Birmingham on behalf of ALSF/English Heritage, Birmingham

Flatman, J & Doeser, J, 2010 The international management of marine aggregates and its relation to maritime archaeology, *The Historic Environment Policy and Practice*, **1**(2), 160–84

Flatman, J & Staniforth, M, 2006 Historical maritime archaeology, in D Hicks & C Beaudry (eds) *Historical archaeology*. Cambridge: Cambridge University Press, ??

Flemming, N, 2002 *The scope of Strategic Environmental Assessment of North Sea areas SEA3 and SEA2 in regard to prehistoric archaeological remains*. London: Department of Trade and Industry

Flemming, N (ed), 2004 *Submarine prehistoric archaeology of the North Sea*, CBA Res Rep **141**. York: Council for British Archaeology

Gaffney, V, Thomson, K & Fitch, S (eds), 2007 *Mapping Doggerland: the Mesolithic landscapes of the southern North Sea*. Oxford: Archaeopress

Gaffney, V, Fitch, S & Smith, D, 2009 *Europe's lost world: the rediscovery of Doggerland*, CBA Res Rep **160**. York: Council for British Archaeology

Gamble, C, 2001 *Archaeology: the basics*. London: Routledge

Gosden, C, 1994 *Social being and time*. Oxford & Cambridge, MA: Blackwell

Gosden, C & Knowles, C, 2001 *Collecting colonialism: material culture and colonial change*. Oxford: Berg

Gupta, S, Collier, J, Parmer-Felgate, A, Dickinson, J, Bushe, K & Humber, S, 2004 Submerged Palaeo-Arun River: reconstruction of prehistoric landscapes and evaluation of archaeological resource potential, ASFL project nos 3543 & 3277, Imperial College on behalf of English Heritage. doi: 10.5284/1000025 Accessed 7 July 2011

Gupta, S, Collier, J, Palmer-Felgate, A & Potter, G, 2007 Catastrophic flooding origin of shelf valley systems in the English Channel, *Nature*, **448**(19), 342–5

Gwyn, D & Palmer, M (eds), 2006 *Understanding the workplace: a research framework for industrial archaeology in Britain*. Leeds: Maney Publishing

Hall, M, 2000 *Archaeology and the modern world: colonial transcripts in South Africa and the Chesapeake*. London: Routledge

Hansom, J D, Lees, G, McGlashan, D J & John, S, 2004 Shoreline Management Plans and coastal cells in Scotland, *Coastal Management*, **32**(3), 227–42

Hegarty, C & Newsome, S, 2007 *Suffolk's defended shore: coastal fortifications from the air*. London: English Heritage and Suffolk County Council

Hillam, J, Groves, C, Brown, D, Baillie, M, Coles, J & Coles, B, 1990 Dendrochronology of the English Neolithic, *Antiquity*, **64**, 210–20

Historic Scotland, 2008 *Historic Scotland framework document 2008*. Edinburgh

Historic Scotland, 2009 *Scottish historic environment policy*. Edinburgh

Historic Scotland, 2010 *The Ancient Monuments and Listed Buildings (Amended) (Scotland) Bill. Consultation and Draft Bill*. Edinburgh

HM Government, 2010a *The Government's statement on the historic environment for England 2010*. London: HMSO

HM Government, 2010b *An initial summary of responses to the UK Marine Policy Statement: a draft for consultation*. London: HMSO Available: http://www.defra.gov.uk/corporate/consult/marine-policy/100721-marine-policy-responses.pdf Accessed 6 July 2011

HM Government, 2010c *Pre-consultation on the draft UK Marine Policy Statement: a paper for discussion*. London: HMSO

HM Goverment 2011 *UK Marine Policy Statement*. London: HMSO

HM Government, Scottish Government, Welsh Assembly Government & Northern Ireland Executive, 2010 *UK Marine Science Strategy*. London: DEFRA on behalf of the Marine Science Co-ordination Committee Available: http://www.defra.gov.uk/publications/2011/04/08/ pb13347-uk-marine-science-strategy/ Accessed 7 July 2011

Hodder, I (ed), 1982 *Symbolic and structural archaeology*. Cambridge: Cambridge University Press

Hodder, I, 1991 Postprocessual archaeology and the current debate, in R Preucel (ed) *Processual and postprocessual archaeologies: multiple ways of knowing the past*. Carbondale, IL: Centre for Archaeological Investigations, Southern Illinois University at Carbondale, 30–41

Hooley, D, 2007 England's historic seascapes – archaeologists look beneath the surface to meet challenges of the ELC, *Landscape Character Network News*, **26**, 8–11

HSE, 1998 *Scientific and archaeological diving projects: Diving at Work Regulations 1997 Approved Code of Practice*, Health & Safety Commission, HSE Books L107. London: HMSO

HWTMA, 2009a Securing a future for marine archaeological archives. Element one: mapping maritime collection areas. Southampton: Hampshire & Wight Trust for Maritime Archaeology

HWTMA, 2009b Securing a future for marine archaeological archives. Element three: analysing present & assessing future archive creation. Southampton: Hampshire & Wight Trust for Maritime Archaeology

HWTMA, 2009c Securing a future for marine archaeological archives. Element two: review of marine archaeological archives and access. Southampton: Hampshire & Wight Trust for Maritime Archaeology

ICOMOS, 1998 International Charter on the Protection and Management of Underwater Cultural Heritage (1996), *Int J Naut Archaeol*, **27**(3), 183–7

IfA, 2001 *Standard and Guidance for Archaeological Desk-based Assessment*. Reading: Institute for Archaeologists

IfA, 2010 *Code of Conduct*. Reading: Institute for Archaeologists

JNAPC, 2008 *Code of Practice for Seabed Development*. JNAPC Available: http://www.jnapc.org. uk/publications.htm Accessed 6 July 2011

JNAPC, 2008 *Code of Practice for Seabed Development*. JNAPC/Crown Estate Available: http:// www.jnapc.org.uk/publications.htm Accessed 6 July 2011

JNAPC, 2010 International shipwrecks. JNAPC Available: http://www.jnapc.org.uk/ International%20shipwrecks.pdf Accessed 6 July 2011

Johnson, M, 2000 *Archaeological theory: an introduction*. Oxford: Blackwell

Kelleher, C, 2007 Quantification of the underwater archaeological resource in Ireland as a means to its management and protection, in J Satchell & P Palma (eds) *Managing the marine cultural heritage: defining, accessing, and managing the resource*, CBA Res Rep **153**. York: Council for British Archaeology, 5–16

Lambeck, K, 1995 Late Devensian and Holocene shorelines of the British Isles and North Sea from models of glacio-hydro-isostatic rebound, *J Geological Soc*, **152**, 437–48

Lawrence, S, 2003 Exporting culture: archaeology and the nineteenth century British Empire, *Historical Archaeology*, **37**(1), 20–33

Lenihan, D, 1983 Rethinking shipwreck archaeology: a history of ideas and considerations for new directions, in R Gould (ed) *Shipwreck anthropology*. Albuquerque, NM: University of New Mexico Press, 37–64

Loveluck, C & Tys, D, 2006 Coastal societies, exchange and identity along the Channel and southern North Sea shore of Europe, AD 600–1000, *J Maritime Archaeol*, **1**, 140–69

Lyell, C, 2005 *Principles of geology* (reprint of 1830–33, with an Introduction by J Secord). London: Penguin Books

Marsden, P, 2003 *Sealed by time: the loss and recovery of the* Mary Rose, The Archaeology of the Mary Rose **1**. Portsmouth: The Mary Rose Trust

Martin, C, 1997 Ships as integrated artefacts: the archaeological potential, in M Redknap (ed) *Artefacts from wrecks: dated assemblages from the late middle ages to the industrial revolution*. Oxford: Oxbow Books, 1–13

McGrail, S, 1995 Romano-Celtic boats and ships: characteristic features, *Int J Naut Archaeol*, **24**(2), 139–45

Merritt, O, 2008 Refining areas of maritime archaeological potential for shipwrecks – AMAP 1 final report. Bournemouth University on behalf of English Heritage

Merritt, O, 2010 AMAP 2 – Characterising the potential for shipwrecks project design. SeaZone on behalf of English Heritage

Merrit, O, 2011 AMAP 2 – Characterising the potential for wrecks. Final Report. SeaZone Solutions Ltd on behalf of English Heritage

Merritt, O, Parham, D & McElvogue, D, 2007 Enhancing our understanding of the marine historic environment: Navigational Hazards Project Final Report. Bournemouth University on behalf of English Heritage

Milne, G A, Mitrovica, J X and Schrag, D P, 2002 Estimating Past Continental Ice Volume from Sea-Level Data. *Quaternary Science Reviews*, **21**, 361–76

Momber, G, 2000 Drowned and deserted: a submerged prehistoric landscape in the Solent, England, *Int J Naut Archaeol*, **29**(1), 86–99

Momber, G, 2004 Drowned and deserted: a submerged prehistoric landscape in the Solent, England, in N Flemming (ed) *Submarine prehistoric archaeology of the North Sea: the inundated landscapes of the Western Solent*, CBA Res Rep **141**. York: Council for British Archaeology, 37–42

Momber, G, 2006 Extracting the cultural heritage: a new challenge for the underwater archaeologist, *Underwater Technology*, **26**(4), 105–11

Momber, G, Satchell, J & Gillespie, J, 2009 Occupation in a submerged Mesolithic landscape, in S McCartan, R Schulting, G Warren & P Woodman (eds) *Mesolithic horizons*. Oxford: Oxbow Books, 324–32

Momber, G, Tomalin, D, Scaife, R, Satchell, J & Gillespie, J, 2011 *Mesolithic occupation at Bouldnor Cliff and the submerged prehistoric landscapes of the Solent*, CBA Res Rep **164**. York: Council for British Archaeology

Moore, H & Wilson, G, 2006 *Report on Coastal Zone Assessment Survey: East Lothian & Scottish Borders*. Edinburgh: EASE Archaeology on behalf of SCAPE Trust and Historic Scotland

Muckelroy, K, 1978 *Maritime archaeology*. Cambridge: Cambridge University Press

Muckelroy, K, 1980 *Archaeology underwater: an atlas of the world's submerged sites*. London: McGraw-Hill Book Company

Murphy, P, 2006 *Shoreline Management Plan Review and the Historic Environment: English Heritage Guidance*. London: English Heritage

Murphy, P, 2007 The submerged prehistoric landscapes of the southern North Sea: work in progress, *Landscapes*, **1**, 1–22

Murphy, P & Trow, S, 2005 Coastal change and the historic environment: building the evidence base, *Conservation Bulletin*, **48**, 8–12

Murphy, P, Thakray, D & Wilson, E, 2009 Coastal heritage and climate change in England: assessing threats and priorities, *Conservation and Management of Archaeological Sites*, **11**(1), 9–15

Nayling, N & Manning, S, 2007 Dating the submerged forests: dendrochronology and radiocarbon 'wiggle-match' dating, In M Bell (ed) *Prehistoric coastal communities: the Mesolithic in western Britain*, CBA Res Rep **149**. York, Council for British Archaeology, 90–102

Olivier, A, 1996 *Frameworks for our past: a review of research frameworks, strategies and perceptions*. London: English Heritage

Oxley, I & O'Regan, D, 2001 *The marine archaeological resource*, IfA Professional Practice Paper **4**. Reading: Institute of Field Archaeologists (http://www.archaeologists.net/publications/papers)

Paddenberg, D & Hession, B, 2008 Underwater archaeology on foot: a systematic rapid foreshore survey on the north Kent coast, England, *Int J Naut Archaeol*, **37**(1), 142–52

Palma, P & Parham, D, 2009 Swash Channel wreck: project report for in situ stabilization of the site. Unpublished report, Bournemouth University on behalf of English Heritage

Parker, A, 1995 Maritime cultures and wreck assemblages in the Graeco-Roman world, *Int J Naut Archaeol*, **24**(2), 87–95

Parker, A, 2001 Maritime landscapes, *Landscapes*, **1**, 22–41

Peeters, H, Murphy, P & Flemming, N (eds), 2009 *North Sea Prehistory Research and Management Framework (NSPRMF) 2009*. Amersfoort: Rijksdienst voor het Cultureel Erfgoed/English Heritage

Penrose, J, 2010 Written response to Parliamentary question tabled by Mr Andrew Smith relating to the future of the Advisory Committee on Historic Wreck Sites. 11th October 2010: Column 219W. www.publications.parliament.uk

Pettitt, P, Gamble, C & Last, J (eds), 2008 *Research and conservation framework for the British Palaeolithic*. The Prehistoric Society & English Heritage

Petts, D & Gerrard, C, 2006 *Shared vision: the North East Regional Research Framework for the Historic Environment*. Durham: Durham County Council

Plets, R, Dix, J & Best, A, 2007 Mapping of the buried Yarmouth Roads wreck, Isle of Wight, UK, using a Chirp Sub-Bottom Profiler, *Int J Naut Archaeol*, **37**(2), 360–73

Quinn, R, Cooper, A & Williams, B, 2000 Marine geophysical investigation of the inshore coastal waters of Northern Ireland, *Int J Naut Archaeol*, **29**, 294–8

Ransley, J, 2007 Rigorous reasoning, reflexive research and the space for 'alternative archaeologies': questions for maritime archaeological heritage management, *Int J Naut Archaeol*, **36**(2), 221–37

Ransley, J, Sturt, F, Dix, J, Adams, J & Blue, L (eds), forthcoming *People and the Sea: A Maritime Archaeological Research Agenda for England*, CBA Research Report **171**. York: Council for British Archaeology

Roberts, P & Trow, S, 2002 *Taking to the water: English Heritage's initial policy for the management of maritime archaeology in England*. London: English Heritage

Rohling, E J, Grant, K, Bolshaw, M, Roberts, A P, Siddall, M, Hemleben, C & Kucera, M, 2009 Antarctic temperature and global sea level closely coupled over the past five glacial cycles, *Nature Geoscience*, **2**, 500–4

Ruppé, C & Barstad, J (eds), 2002 *International handbook of underwater archaeology*. London/New York: Plenum Press

Shennan, I & Andrews, J, 2000 *Holocene land–ocean interaction and environmental change around the North Sea*, Geological Society Special Publication **166**. London

Shennan, I, Bradley, S, Milne, G, Brooks, A, Bassett, S & Hamilton, S, 2006 Relative sea-level changes, glacial isostatic modelling and ice-sheet reconstructions from the British Isles since the Last Glacial Maximum. *J Quaternary Sci* **21**, 585–99

Staniforth, M, 2003 *Material culture and consumer society: dependent colonies in colonial Australia*. New York: Kluwer Academic/Plenum Publishers

The Crown Estate, 2010 *Protocol for Archaeological Discoveries. Offshore Renewables Projects*. London: Wessex Archaeology on behalf of The Crown Estate. Available: http://www.thecrownestate.co.uk/media/122838/pad offshore renewables.pdf Accessed 14 January 2012

The Scottish Government, 2010 *Scottish planning policy*. Edinburgh

Tilley, C, 1989 Interpreting material culture, in I Hodder (ed) *The meaning of things: material culture and symbolic expression*. London: Unwin Hyman, 185–94

Tilley, C (ed), 1990 *Reading material culture*. Cambridge: Basil Blackwell

Tilley, C (ed), 1993 *Interpretative archaeology*. Oxford: Berg Publishers

Tomalin, D, 2000 Palaeo-environmental investigations of submerged sediment archives in the West Solent study area at Bouldnor and Yarmouth, in R McInnes, D Tomalin & J Jakeways (eds) *Coastal change, climate and instability*, European Commission LIFE project. Ventnor: Isle of Wight Council, 13–45

UN, 1983 *United Nations convention on the law of the sea*. New York: United Nations

UNESCO, 2001 *Convention on the protection of the underwater cultural heritage*. Available: http://unesdoc.unesco.org/images/0012/001260/126065e.pdf Accessed 6 July 2011

Watson, P J, 1983 Method and theory in shipwreck archaeology, in R Gould (ed) *Shipwreck anthropology*. Albuquerque, NM: Albuquerque Press, 23–36

Wessex Archaeology, 2007 *Historic environment guidance for the offshore renewable energy sector*. London: Wessex Archaeology Ltd on behalf of COWRIE (www.offshorewind.co.uk)

Wessex Archaeology, 2008 *Aircraft crash sites at sea: a scoping study. archaeological desk-based assessment*. Salisbury: Wessex Archaeology on behalf of English Heritage

Westerdahl, C, 1992 The maritime cultural landscape, *Int J Naut Archaeol*, **21**(1), 5–14

Westerdahl, C, 1994 Maritime cultures and ships types: brief comments on the significance of maritime archaeology, *Int J Naut Archaeol*, **23**(4), 265–70

Whitewright, J & Satchell, J (eds), 2011 *The archaeology and history of the* Flower of Ugie, *wrecked 1852 in the Eastern Solent*, HWTMA Monograph series **1**. Oxford: BAR British series **511**

Williams, B, 2001 Commercial developments and their impact on maritime heritage: the Northern Ireland experience, *Int J Naut Archaeol*, **30**(1), 5–11

Williams, M, Underwood, C, Bowens, A, Dromgoole, S, Firth, A *et al*, 2005 Marine archaeology legislation project. Wolverhampton: University of Wolverhampton on behalf of English Heritage. Available: www.jnapc.org.uk/MALP.pdf Accessed 7 July 2011

Willis, S, 2009 The archaeology of smuggling and the Falmouth King's Pipe, *J Maritime Archaeol*, **4**, 51–65

Index

Entries in bold refer to the Figures

foreshore, the 5, 19, 62
    ownership of 4
funding 18, 24, 28, 32, 42, 44, 52, 74

Gagnan, Emile 10
geology 39
geomorphology 28
geophysical survey 19, 25, 34, 38, 39, 40, 44, 73
geotechnical survey data 38
glacial models 19
government, UK, role in protecting cultural
    heritage 23, 24, 80
ground truthing 25, 70

habitation remains 13 see also archaeological
    remains, marine; human settlement;
    prehistoric archaeological remains
Halley, Edmund 7
Hampshire and Wight Trust for Maritime
    Archaeology (HWTMA) 21, 28, 43–4
    Eastern Solent Marine Archaeology
        Project 43
health and safety 41–2
Health and Safety Executive, the 41
heritage agencies 16, 39–40, 46, 50, 57, 71, 73
    see also Cadw; English Heritage; Historic
    Scotland
heritage assets see historic assets
'heritage cycle' 46, **47**
Heritage Gateway 36
Heritage Protection Bill (draft) 61, 62–3
high seas, the 3, 79
historic assets 3, 10, 14, 23, 25, 35, 69
    finite nature of 6, 21, 24, 91
historic charts and surveys 37
historic environment, the 'significance' of 65,
    66, 75
Historic Environment Guidance for the Offshore
    Renewable Energy Sector 34
Historic Environment Local Management
    (HELM) 95
Historic Environment Records (HERs) 26,
    36, 70
Historic Landscape Characterisation (HLC)
    83, 85–6
Historic Marine Protection Areas 61–2, 64,
    94
Historic Scotland 18, 52, 59
Historic Seascape Characterisation (HSC)
    77, 84–6
Historic Wales 36
Historical Diving Society 10
historical documentation 12

HMS Colossus 40
Holocene, the 20, 39
human migration and dispersal 29, 90
human remains 26
human settlement 29
hydrographic material 37

ICOMOS 11
    Charter on the Protection and Management
        of Underwater Cultural Heritage 11
industries, marine sector 24, 70
Institute of Archaeologists (IfA) 14, 32–3, 39, 53
    Code of Conduct 33
    Maritime Affairs Group 16, 24, 53–4
    Standards and Guidance for Archaeological
        Desk-based Assessment 34
international conventions relating to
    underwater cultural heritage 2, 77
International Journal of Nautical Archaeology
    10, 54
intertidal zone 1, 35, 36, 50, 63, 84, 94
Ireland 25
Irish Sea, the 28, 73

jetsam 60, 94
Joint Nautical Archaeology Policy Committee
    (JNAPC) 24, 53, 55
    Code of Practice for Seabed Development
        34, 70
Journal of Maritime Archaeology 81

La Surveillante 40
lagan 60, 94
land/sea interface, 'seamless' approach to 13,
    46, 60, 62, 63, 67, 77, 86
Le Prieur, Yves 9
legislation
    relating to shipwrecks 49, 51, 54
    relating to underwater cultural heritage 2,
        16, 9, 54–5, 57–9, 75
libraries 37
listing, of historic buildings 51, 62
local archives 37–8
log boats 45
Lyell, Charles 10

McKee, Alexander 12
'Mapping Navigational Hazards as Areas of
    Maritime Archaeological Potential' project
    42
Marine Accident Investigation Branch 42
marine aggregates, extraction of 5, 25, 73–4 see
    also aggregate producers

Other titles in the Council for British Archaeology's Practical Handbook series:

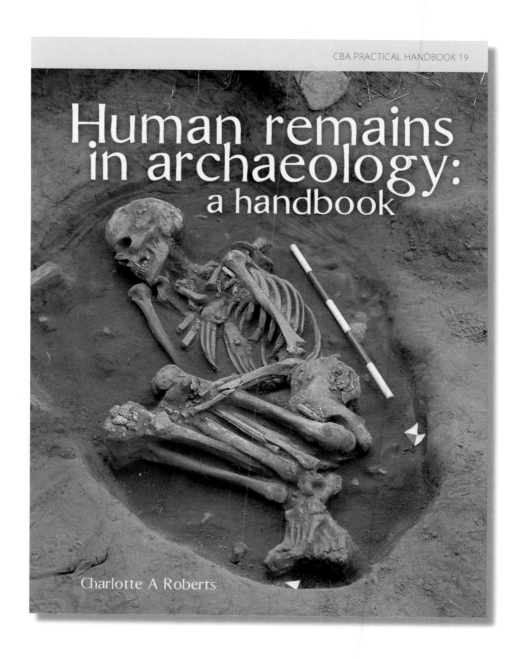

CBA PRACTICAL HANDBOOK 19

Human remains in archaeology:
a handbook

Charlotte A Roberts

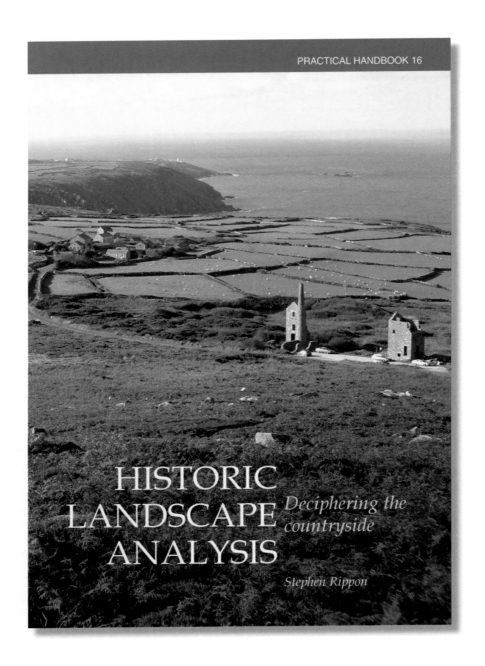

HISTORIC LANDSCAPE ANALYSIS

Deciphering the countryside

Stephen Rippon

For more information about Council for British Archaeology publications, visit: www.archaeologyUK.org

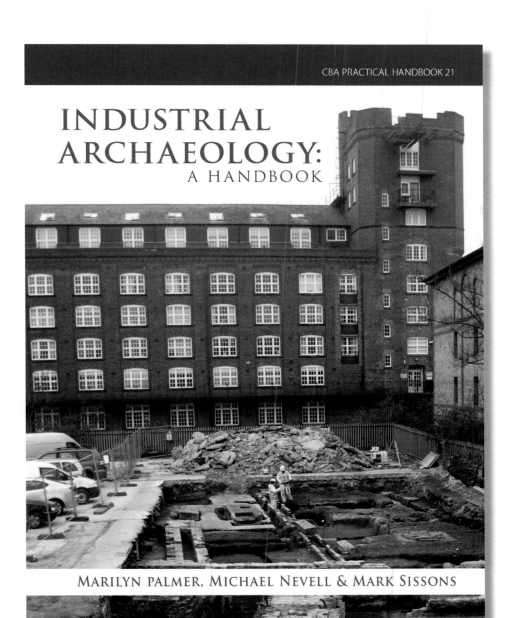

INDUSTRIAL ARCHAEOLOGY:
A HANDBOOK

MARILYN PALMER, MICHAEL NEVELL & MARK SISSONS

For more information about Council for British Archaeology publications, visit: www.archaeologyUK.org

FIXTURES AND FITTINGS IN DATED HOUSES 1567-1763

drawings by Linda Hall   text by N W Alcock and Linda Hall

PRACTICAL HANDBOOK IN ARCHAEOLOGY 11

**RECORDING TIMBER-FRAMED BUILDINGS:
AN ILLUSTRATED GLOSSARY**

N W Alcock, M W Barley, P W Dixon and R A Meeson
Illustrations by R A Meeson

PRACTICAL HANDBOOK IN ARCHAEOLOGY 5

For more information about Council for
British Archaeology publications,
visit: www.archaeologyUK.org